Miracles,
Demons,
and Spiritual
Warfare

Miracles, Demons, and Spiritual Warfare

An Urgent Call for Discernment

Edward N. Gross

BAKER BOOK HOUSE
Grand Rapids, Michigan 49516

Copyright 1990 by Baker Book House

Third printing, January 1991

Printed in the United States of America

Library of Congress Cataloging-in-Publication Data

Gross, Edward N.
   Miracles, Demons, and Spiritual Warfare; an urgent call for discernment / Edward N. Gross.
       p. cm.
     ISBN 0-8010-3835-9
     1. Miracles. 2. Apologetics—20th century. 3. Gifts, Spiritual.
4. Demonology. I. Title.
BT97.2.G76 1990   89-38804
231.7′3—dc20   CIP

It is with deepest love and gratitude that I dedicate this book to my wife, Debby, my faithful helper, wisest counselor, and most trusted friend.

Contents

**Part Three   Defeating Demons
                and Discerning True Faith**

Appendixes

Foreword

Miracles, demons, spiritual warfare—these and related themes have always been on the agenda of the church and its missions. However, they are higher on the agenda today than at any time in recent history. Why? Probably for several reasons.

In the first place, overt witchcraft, spirit worship, Satan worship, and the like until recently have not been part of the experience of most Christians in the Western world. Only as missionaries have reported their experiences among faraway and more "primitive" peoples have we given such phenomena serious consideration. More recently, however, both the Christian and secular press—and often personal experience as well—have made us aware of the fact that Satan is the "god of this age," not only in remote times and places, but also in our own neighborhoods and right now!

Secondly, the rapid rise of the Pentecostal and charismatic movements in the twentieth century has occasioned a reassessment of the nature of the work of the Holy Spirit, the identification of spiritual gifts, and the place of signs and wonders in the economy of God. Tongues speaking, physical healings, and exorcisms have been widely reported, not only among traditional Pentecostals but also across an ecclesiastical spectrum that includes Episcopalians and Roman Catholics. One television preacher recently exhorted his congregation, "Don't tell people that we pray for the sick. Tell them that we *heal* them!"

Thirdly, the concept and strategy of "power encounter" has now become very prominent, particularly in missionary theory and practice. One of the first to use the term was the Methodist missiologist Alan Tippett who introduced it in his book *Verdict Theology* published in 1969. Since that time articles, seminars, and courses in "power encounter" have attracted ever-increasing attention and participation. Some people define "power encounter" very narrowly in terms of overt and dramatic demonstrations of the fact that Christ is more powerful than false gods and spirits. Others relate it more broadly to the spiritual warfare that is always and everywhere a part of Christian living and ministry. In either case, the place of miraculous demonstrations of divine power today becomes the focus of discussion.

It is understandable that in such a climate many people, both believers and unbelievers, are troubled by numerous and basic questions having to do with a whole range of miraculous phenomena. Are miracles for today? Is tongues speaking an evidence of Spirit baptism? Are any of those reported healings really genuine? How can we distinguish between, for example, psychological depression and spiritual oppression? Can believers be demon-possessed? Which ones—if any—of the faith healers are "for real"? And so on.

Unfortunately, such questions quite regularly engender more heat than light. "Proofs" of genuineness or deceitfulness, of credibility or charlatanry, revolve around the answers to such data as the relationship between "tongues" and the structure of known languages, or the conclusions of prominent physicians and psychologists. Proponents on both sides of such questions examine the evidence, come to different conclusions, and then promote their conclusion with more passion than reason.

Secularists can hardly be expected to place much stock in a study of the Bible when it comes to resolving such questions. But the Scripture should constitute the primary resource for true Christians. We have every reason for believing that the witness of Holy Spirit-inspired Scripture on the one hand, and the witness of Holy Spirit-empowered ministry on the other will not contradict each other but rather will reinforce each other. *Ultimately, both the validity of our conclusions regarding supernatural gifts and miracles, and the effectiveness of our warfare against the Evil One should be tested, not on the basis of competing claims and human arguments, but on the basis of "thus saith the Lord."*

That brings us to the importance of this book. Dr. Gross's first concern is to discover what the Bible says concerning these matters and to set forth those teachings in an understandable and forthright manner. It is not to be expected that all Christians will be persuaded by his arguments, though many will. But at least three things will happen to those who carefully read and consider what he has written. First, they will be better instructed in subjects that promise to be of increasing concern to the church and its missions. Second, they will be encouraged to "search the Scriptures" more diligently in a day when confusion is often the rule rather than the exception. And third, they will be motivated to give greater glory to the Triune God, the Source of all truth and power. More than that can hardly be expected of any book, so I congratulate the author for writing it and commend it to all inquiring Christians for their reading and edification.

David J. Hesselgrave
Trinity Evangelical Divinity School

Preface

Jesus repeatedly asked Peter, "Lovest thou me?" After each of the apostle's responses, the Lord commanded Peter to feed "my lambs" and "my sheep" (John 21:15–18). I think that Jesus asked Peter this question three times, not so much because Peter denied him thrice, but because of the importance of the question itself. It is imperative that we, too, should seek proper ways to manifest our love to our precious Savior. The best way is simply by obeying him. "He that hath my commandments, and keepeth them, he it is that loveth me" (John 14:21a). When we all do our duty, cheerfully as unto the Lord, in whatever place he has been pleased to put us, we truly reveal love to him. To those whom Christ has called as shepherds in his Church, one indispensable way to manifest love to him is by feeding his flock.

This conviction has motivated me to write. I love Christ and want to prove my love by feeding his sheep. He views as done to himself those deeds done in love to his children. "Inasmuch as ye have done it unto one of the least of these my brethren, ye have done it unto me" (Matt. 25:40).

Paul warned of "grievous wolves" entering the church "not sparing the flock" (Acts 20:29). That was not simply a first-century phenomenon. The flock is also being ravaged today.

11

One of the avenues through which the devil and his dupes are presently attacking the tender lambs of Christ involves miracles. Unfortunately, sides are being hastily taken and salvos are being immediately shot before the issue has been objectively studied in the light of Scripture. Only after such study can error be properly identified. Every effort should be expended to discover what the captain of our salvation has said through his inerrant Word.

In dealing with this topic I have had to mention various names. One person often referred to is John Wimber. In my opinion, John Wimber represents the best of evangelistic concerns united with some of the worst of current theological beliefs. Although mixture of truth and error is extremely dangerous, we are not warranted to hastily defame Wimber as some self-serving magician. There are tremendous weaknesses in his position, but insincerity, greed, and willful deception are not among them. Our position is never strengthened by unfairly representing those with whom we disagree.

Complex issues concerning miracles, spiritual gifts, demonization, extrabiblical revelation, and power encounter are addressed in this book. Biblical consistency is the chief aim, for what good is a position which either ignores or contradicts truth? The position presented here is not new. Many Christians have wrestled with these issues and come to conclusions similar to those which I have drawn.

I have attempted to deal with these difficult issues without increasing the present polarization between Christians. Indeed, it is my hope that God would use this work to instruct, heal and unite divided Christians around a consistent interpretation of his holy Word.

The readers will immediately notice my heavy indebtedness to the great old Princeton theologians Archibald Alexander, Charles and A. A. Hodge, B. B. Warfield, and J. Gresham Machen. I have found in the lives and writings of these men the best of evangelistic concerns united with the best of theological beliefs. My attempts to feed Christ's flock have been tremendously furthered by the writings of these men who so faithfully served the church in their day. And I heartily recommend their writings to any Christian longing to grow in the knowledge of God's Word. In them you will find what Paul called "wholesome words" and "doctrine which is according to godliness" (1 Tim. 6:3).

Realizing the spiritual impoverishment of our day, and the great assistance the old Princeton theologians can be in today's theological training, the administration of Biblical Theological Seminary (200 N. Main Street, Hatfield, PA 19440 Phone: 215-368-5000) presents, as a part of its program, courses developed from these astute Christians.

I would be delighted to receive any response which the reader might have to this book.

Dr. Edward N. Gross
PO Box 11288
Elkins Park, PA 19117

Defining
Biblical
Parameters

1

What Are
Miracles

?

A little while ago I was watching one of the better-known television preachers. He began the telecast by promising to report a great miracle that had recently taken place in his ministry. After no small amount of drama, he explained that a company near his complex had decided to sell a very large building. This building was greatly needed by the Christian ministry he had founded. Its becoming available he constantly affirmed to be a miracle. On that same broadcast the preacher began a drive to raise the money to purchase the miracle building for millions of dollars.

Here was a highly respected minister declaring that God had worked a miracle. There was no extravagant claim by the minister that he was the agent who had produced it, but he dogmatically insisted that it was a miracle. Was it a miracle? Is there any danger in calling this a miracle? Just what is a miracle? Is Dennis Bennett right when he says, "Miracles are usually small things. . . . A parking place when needed is quite a

17

common miracle, and can be a very significant one in a crowded city at rush hour!" (Hamilton 1975, 17)?

A great theologian, Benjamin B. Warfield (1851–1921), wrote, "One would think it a principle too obvious to require insisting upon that every discussion of miracles should begin with a clearly defined conception of what a miracle is and what is asserted to have occurred when it is affirmed that a miracle has taken place" (Warfield 1976, 167).

It would greatly benefit us all if this simple rule were followed. Unfortunately, it rarely is. How can profit result from a discussion involving terms that are not understood? Yet Christians constantly say, "It's a miracle!" without understanding what they are affirming. Is it a miracle when we run out of gas so near to a gas station that we coast right up to the pump? Or when we receive an unexpected gift? Or when we grab our child just before the swing hits him in the head? These are all reasons for thanking the Lord, but should they be called miracles? No, they should not.

The relationship of miracles to Christianity is a matter of extreme importance. When the Lord works directly, apart from human agency, he reveals himself with utmost clarity. All intervening clouds are temporarily removed. And the almighty God is glorified in the sight of his admiring creatures. This is not the outcome, though, when an event caused by human agency is termed a miracle. Such declarations rob God of the glory and honor due to him alone.

An accurate definition of the term, then, is a matter of primary concern. We must not let our emotions run away with us when we are describing the wonderful providences that God weaves into our lives each day. Wrong definitions lead to wrong conclusions, even when they are made by sincere, well-intentioned Christians. The cause of God and truth are not served by a definition of miracles that in any way confuses the works of God with the works wrought either by the power of men or by some unknown force. Where are we to look for an accurate definition? The logical place to find a definition of

God's unique acts is in the revelation made by God himself. So we must investigate the Bible, God's holy Word.

The Biblical Foundation

The psalmist said, "The entrance of thy words giveth light; it giveth understanding unto the simple" (Ps. 119:130). The Bible is a revelation of truth. Jesus said, "Thy word is truth" (John 17:17). It is most unwise, then, to depart from its teachings when searching for spiritual truth. Because "all Scripture is given by inspiration of God" it "is profitable for doctrine" according to 2 Timothy 3:16. What is profitable should be followed. The divine inspiration of the Bible is not just in the ideas revealed, as some affirm, but in the exact language employed. Its very words are inspired of God. This is proven by these direct statements in Scripture:

> Every word of God is pure: he is a shield unto them that put their trust in him. Add thou not unto his words, lest he reprove thee, and thou be found a liar (Prov. 30:5, 6).
>
> But he answered and said, It is written, Man shall not live by bread alone, but by every word that proceedeth out of the mouth of God (Matt. 4:4 quoting Deut. 8:3).

The verbal inspiration of Scripture is also evidenced from the fact that inspired men defend their teaching by referring to single words used in the Scriptures (see John 10:34–36; Gal. 3:16). This could not be done unless the specific words were breathed by God.

We are living in the age of paraphrasing. Fewer and fewer people contend that we ought to use the very words of Scripture when teaching or translating the Bible. But this seems potentially dangerous if the very words are inspired, because when paraphrasing occurs we are removed another level from the inspired, original words. This is true when speaking about any biblical truth, whether it be miracles, justification, sanctification, or election. A great nineteenth-century theologian of

Princeton Seminary, Charles Hodge, emphasized the importance of representing theological truth in its biblical form. He warned: "As this is the Scriptural mode of representation, it is of great importance that it should be retained in theology. Our only security for retaining the truths of the Bible, is to adhere to the Scriptures as closely as possible in our mode of presenting the doctrines therein revealed" (C. Hodge 1960, vol. 3, p. 355).

Some authors have forgotten this principle when discussing miracles. This is done by those who term every unusual, unplanned event a miracle. It is also done by those who affirm that only God works miracles, disregarding the fact of satanic miracles. Whereas our topic is one of the most difficult in the whole study of theology, Christians today should understand what Scripture teaches concerning miracles. Our God is a God of truth. He is not glorified by us when we choose either to modify his Word or to ignore it. As we unfold our discussion, it is vital that we stick closely to the specific words of Scripture.

The Biblical Definition

Miracles are superhuman events. They are wrought by a power greater than what mere humans possess. The New Testament normally describes miracles by three terms: signs, wonders, and mighty works (or power). Usually just one of these terms is chosen to describe a miracle. The word *sign* is often used alone, as in Matthew 12:38 and John 20:30. In Mark 6:5 the words *mighty work* stand alone, signifying a miracle. *Wonders* also occurs alone, as in Acts 2:19. Sometimes two of the terms are linked together, such as *signs and wonders* (Acts 4:30; 5:12; 7:36). Occasionally all three terms are joined, as in 2 Corinthians 12:12: "Truly the signs of an apostle were wrought among you in all patience, in signs, and wonders, and mighty deeds" (see also Acts 2:22). So the true nature of a miracle is not completely described by any one of these terms individually, but by all of them when used collectively. Each one of these terms describes the miracle from a different perspective.

Signs

Miracles are called signs around sixty times in the Greek New Testament. This word is chosen to identify a miracle because it distinguishes the person performing the miracle to be the authorized messenger of a superior power. A sign is an emblem of identification. A road sign identifies the condition of the highway just ahead. This is what miracles did. They identified their performers as the empowered representatives of a superhuman power. Sometimes this power was God (as in John 2:11; 3:2; 20:30; Heb. 2:4). Sometimes this power was Satan (2 Thess. 2:9; Rev. 19:20) or demons (Rev. 16:14).

The Jews often approached Jesus and "required a sign" of him. They did the same to his apostles. In other words, they demanded them to perform a miracle on the spot, which would so amaze those present that all doubt would be removed from their minds. This demand was constantly resisted by the Lord (see Mark 8:11, 12). Jesus knew that performing a miracle was no reliable proof of one's divine mission, nor would miracles alone prove this. Satan can be "transformed into an angel of light" in our sight (2 Cor. 11:14). "Therefore it is no great thing if his ministers also be transformed as the ministers of righteousness" (2 Cor. 11:15). They have always been able to perform miracles (see Exodus 7:10–12, 20–22; 8:6, 7).

So the sign, standing alone, does not give us infallible certainty that an individual is representing the true and living God. Satan is delighted when a mere display of power is made the criterion of the authenticity of a man's mission. This he can counterfeit. But there are other distinguishing marks of God's representatives that he cannot duplicate. We will study these at a later time.

Wonders

Miracles were called wonders because of the effects they produced on the witnesses. Something was done that totally amazed the beholders. A wonder had to be something apart from normal human agency and experience. In the Greek New Testament this word is used sixteen times. It depicts the miracles of God in the Old Testament (Acts 7:36), of Jesus (Acts 2:22), of the apostles (Acts 2:43; 5:12; Heb. 2:4), of Stephen (Acts 6:8), and of the workers of Satan (Matt. 24:24; Mark 13:22; 2 Thess. 2:9). Since wonders can be performed by Satan, working wonders only cannot be a sure evidence that the performer is of God.

The use of this word in describing a miracle leads us to another important conclusion: the very nature of a miracle demands that it be an unusual or uncommon event wrought in the sight of an audience. There are those today who affirm that their miracle-working gifts are often displayed through their ministries. But where are the wonders? Where are the obvious, outward, verifiable evidences of the immediate power of God? A miracle is visible or verifiable. How pathetic are most claims of miracles today! People insist that they feel better after being prayed for. This might be true, but it is not a wonder. Through Christ the blind saw, the crippled walked, the deaf heard. And these were all verified by friends or family who knew the previous condition. Now, these were true wonders glorifying God. And real wonders today must be wrought under similar circumstances.

When miracles become commonplace, they lose their uniqueness. Read Psalm 78:10–33. The Israelites witnessed miracle after miracle, but with little lasting impression. The devil has effectively led many astray by his miracles for this very reason: he does not perform them so often as to make them commonplace events. Hence, the automatic assumption that many wrongly have made when experiencing a miracle is that it must be from God.

Western countries such as the United States and Canada are particularly susceptible to this deception. The enormous advancements made through scientific and industrial technology have all come through human agency. Materialism has become

the god of the West. This has left Westerners spiritually im-
poverished. Hence, many churches have been transformed into
social institutions where God's power is rarely felt and never
seen. There has developed an enormous "power vacuum." The
only power experienced by many in the West is physical power.
This is most unfulfilling to us, because we are spiritual as well
as physical beings.

Today there is every evidence of an enormous resurgence of
interest in the spiritual world. The unbridled pursuit of wealth
and sex has devastated our society. Multitudes are fed up, but
do not know where to turn. Adultery, drugs, AIDS, divorce,
child abuse, lawlessness are all ravaging our country. Parents
are searching for help. Spiritual awareness is increasing. Spiritual power is craved. And Satan is flooding the West with his
counterfeits. The New Age movement offers spiritual power.
There are real "wonders" to behold in Satan's counterfeits.
Transchanneling is bringing increased thousands of spiritually
starved people into contact with the world of demons. And it is
a world of power. But what good is power if it does not lead
people to God?

Mighty Deeds

Miracles in the Scriptures are also termed mighty deeds
(works of power) some twenty-eight times. This Greek word
views the miracle simply from the perspective of power. The real
source was always superhuman. Jesus performed mighty
works (Matt. 11:20; Luke 19:37; Acts 10:38), as did the
apostles (Luke 9:1; Acts 19:11; 2 Cor. 12:12), some Christians
(1 Cor. 12:10, 29), and the servants of Satan (Matt. 7:22; Acts
8:10; Rev. 13:2–4). The things that these agents performed
were beyond the unaided ability of human beings. Miracles
demand a power source higher than what mankind possesses.
But since Scripture portrays evil men working mighty deeds,
we must conclude that raw, miracle-working power alone does
not authenticate its agent as the spokesman of God.

Let us return to the claim of the preacher mentioned in the

beginning of this chapter. The building becoming available was a wonderful answer to prayer. It was a gracious act of God's providence. But it was not a miracle. It was not a sign, wonder, or mighty deed. To term it a miracle is to cheapen true miracles wrought by God's power. This is a very mild example of what is going on today. Far greater claims can be heard daily on radio and television. Christians seem to be competing in an attempt to top each others' miracles. When one compares the vast majority of these "miracles" with those of the New Testament, today's sink into oblivion, utterly unworthy of belonging to the same class of events that accompanied Christ and the apostles.

Where is the discernment among Christians today? Do our leaders have to claim the working of miracles in order to have their ministries acceptable to us? Do such alleged miracles automatically transform people into worthy leaders and teachers? Have Christians lost all ability to distinguish between presumption and faith? Is that person closest to God whose statements are the most daring and alarming? No! Such blatant sensationalism robs Christianity of its glory and goodness, transforming its adherents from humble servants into pretentious showmen.

The topic of miracles is no trifling matter. Confusion here could result in disaster. The devil is a master of deceit. This fact combined with the limitations of human knowledge concerning miracles increases the possibility of deception. We need all the help available to aid us in making correct assessments concerning miracles. Christ warned that the day is coming when false prophets "shall show great signs and wonders; so as to lead astray, if possible, even the elect" (Matt. 24:24 ASV). I fear that today's ignorance concerning miracles is paving the way for a future apostasy of staggering proportions, as prophesied in the following passage:

> Let no man deceive you by any means: for that day shall not come, except there come a falling away first, and that man of sin

be revealed, the son of perdition. . . . Even him, whose coming is after the working of Satan with all power and signs and lying wonders, and with all deceivableness of unrighteousness in them that perish; because they received not the love of the truth, that they might be saved" (2 Thess. 2:3, 9, 10).

2

Why Did
Miracles Occur
in Old Testament Times

?

Now that we better understand what a miracle is, we must investigate the purpose of miracles. Why does God work miracles? What is his design in performing these glorious acts? Or are they arbitrary events without distinct purpose?

The psalmist declares, "But our God is in the heavens: he hath done whatsoever he hath pleased" (Ps. 115:3). God works according to his eternal plan, with every single event woven into the fabric of history according to his infinite wisdom. Even the falling of a sparrow is included in his divine plan (Matt. 10:29). If the seemingly insignificant events in life are part of this plan, even more so are the great events. Even "the king's heart is in the hands of the LORD, as the rivers of water: he turneth it whithersoever he will" (Prov. 21:1). Miracles are certainly great events. They are not meaningless interruptions in human history. They have a divine purpose. Those miracles that are wrought by God have been specially designed by him to accomplish definite ends. And the Bible does not leave its readers guessing what the design of miracles is. It specifically reveals why they occur.

The Old Testament consists of thirty-nine inspired books of God. Miracles did not happen very commonly during the Old Testament era. In fact, most of the miracles mentioned in the Old Testament occurred in three periods. John D. Davis notes these epochs as follows:

> 1. The redemption of God's people from Egypt and their establishment in Canaan under Moses and Joshua. 2. The life and death struggle of the true religion with heathenism under Elijah and Elisha. 3. The exile, when Jehovah afforded proof of his power and supremacy over the gods of the heathen, although his people were in captivity (Daniel and his companions) (Davis 1973, 527).

The Mosaic era took place during the fifteenth century B.C. The era of Elijah and Elisha was the ninth century B.C. And Daniel lived in captivity during the sixth century B.C. The Bible states something specific about the purpose of miracles in all three of these periods.

The First Epoch of Miracles

Moses was concerned that the Israelites would not believe that he was truly sent from God (Exod. 4:1–5). He said to God, "But, behold, they will not believe me, nor hearken unto my voice: for they will say, The LORD hath not appeared unto thee." The Lord responded by asking him a question: "What is that in thine hand?" Moses replied, "A rod." The Lord told Moses to cast it on the ground, which Moses did, "and it became a serpent." Moses was certain that the rod had become a snake, because he "fled from before it." This was a miracle.

Why did God perform this miracle and then give Moses the authority to duplicate it? The answer is given by the Lord: "That they may believe that the LORD God of their fathers, the

God of Abraham, the God of Isaac, and the God of Jacob, hath appeared unto thee" (Exod. 4:5). He then gave Moses another sign (4:6, 7), stating, "And it shall come to pass, if they will not believe thee, neither hearken to the voice of the first sign, that they will believe the voice of the latter sign" (4:8). So these miracles were designed to convince the Israelites that Moses was a prophet of God bearing the message of God to them.

The great Protestant Reformer John Calvin (1509–1564) wrote:

> Moses is armed with power from heaven to make his voca-tion sure, and that no one may doubt him to be a Prophet divinely commissioned. It would be out of place here to com-prehensively detail the use of miracles, suffice it briefly to lay down, that they sometimes serve as preparatives to faith, some-times for its confirmation (Calvin 1984 2:A:87).

Moses could perform these miracles because such would help authenticate him as an inspired prophet or messenger of God. It helped prepare or strengthen the faith of the children of Israel, so they would follow the word of God as spoken by Moses.

The many miracles that accompanied the Israelites' redemp-tion from Egyptian bondage were purposed chiefly to exalt or glorify God. The Lord said to Pharaoh, "And in very deed for this cause have I raised thee up, for to show in thee my power; and that my name may be declared throughout all the earth" (Exod. 9:16). The reign and resistance of Pharaoh were allowed by God that through them he might gloriously reveal his power over all things, his love to his people, and his justice in punish-ing sin (see Rom. 9:17, 22, 23).

The Second Epoch of Miracles

Elijah was God's prophet in a day of dark apostasy. The showdown with the prophets of Baal took place on Mount Car-mel. The children of Israel were floundering in their faith. Who was the true God? Who was a true prophet? These were the burning issues of the day. How was this impasse to be resolved? It was agreed that "the God that answereth by fire, let him be God" (1 Kings 18:24). The prophets of Baal were unsuccessful. Then Elijah called on the Lord for a miracle. What was the purpose of the miracle? Elijah's own words supply the answer: "LORD God of Abraham, Isaac, and of Israel, let it be known this day that thou art God in Israel, and that I am thy servant, and that I have done all these things at thy word" (1 Kings 18:36).

Elijah saw the miracle as performing two basic functions: the vindication of Jehovah's deity and of his prophet's ministry.

The circumstances involving the widow of Zarephath and the death of her son furnish another clear example of the purpose of miracles. She had interpreted her son's death as God's judgment on her for past sins (1 Kings 17:18). So when the Lord used Elijah in raising her dead son, she understood that the Lord was a merciful and loving God. He had forgiven her. His gracious nature was exalted by the miracle. The widow declared, "Now by this I know that thou art a man of God, and that the word of the LORD in thy mouth is truth" (v. 24). The miracle also verified Elijah as a true prophet of the Lord.

The Third Epoch of Miracles

God's judgment fell on Judah through the destruction of Nebuchadnezzar. Daniel was taken captive during this Babylonian captivity. The Lord miraculously exalted himself and protected his children during this era. Time after time the message and faith of the prophet Daniel were vindicated by miracles.

The dream of Nebuchadnezzar provides one instance of God's mighty power. None of Babylon's wise men could interpret the dream, so the king ordered all of them to be killed. Daniel and his friends "[desired] mercies of the God of heaven concerning this secret; that Daniel and his fellows should not perish with the rest of the wise men of Babylon" (Dan. 2:18).

God miraculously answered their prayers by providing the meaning of the dream. As Daniel appeared before Nebuchadnezzar, he said: "The secret which the king hath demanded cannot the wise men, the astrologers, the magicians, the soothsayers, shew unto the king; but there is a God in heaven that revealeth secrets, and maketh known to king Nebuchadnezzar what shall be in the latter days" (Dan. 2:27, 28).

On Daniel's revealing the meaning of the king's dream, "The king answered unto Daniel, and said, Of a truth it is, that your God is a God of gods, and a LORD of kings, and a revealer of secrets, seeing thou couldest reveal this secret" (2:47; also 4:2, 3, 34, 35). Because of the miracle God was glorified and his servants were spared from death.

Later, King Darius declared:

> I make a decree, that in every dominion of my kingdom men tremble and fear before the God of Daniel: for he is the living God, and stedfast forever, and his kingdom that which shall not be destroyed, and his dominion shall be even unto the end. He delivereth and rescueth, and he worketh signs and wonders in heaven and in earth, who hath delivered Daniel from the power of the lions (Dan. 6:26, 27).

In the Old Testament, then, there is often a close connection between miracles and the prophets of God. Psalm 74:9 reveals that miraculous signs and the ministry of prophets were inextricably united in the minds of Old Testament believers. "We see not our signs: there is no more any prophet." Why was there need for prophets to work miracles? A. A. Hodge (1823–1886) answers:

> If God directly intervenes to instruct and educate his children, revelations and miracles must cooperate in that work. Each prophet sent to speak for God must be authenticated. Men sent bearing supernatural messages will reasonably be expected to possess supernatural phenomena (A. Hodge 1976, 56).

There was a definite purpose, then, for the occurrence of

miracles in the ministries of God's prophets. These miracles were their credentials. Miracles vindicated the claims of these men that they were divinely commissioned to reveal God's word to humankind. Those today who claim to speak as prophets of God with direct revelation from him must prove their claim in the same incontestable manner.

But we have seen that, although an important purpose of miracles was to authenticate a prophet of God, this was not the only design. God manifesting himself to his creatures, glorifying his divine nature, is always paramount in those miraculous events which he enacts. Warfield agrees, stating that the relation of special revelation to "miracles has often been very unnecessarily confused by one-sided statements. Miracles are not merely credentials of revelation, but vehicles of revelation as well; . . . they are inevitably revelatory of God" (Warfield 1981, 1:47).

Miracles reveal the nature of God. This is their chief design: to glorify God. His love is seen in delivering his children from Sennacherib's army (Isa. 37) or from a fiery furnace (Dan. 3). His holiness and justice are magnified through miracles of judgment, such as with Lot's wife (Gen. 19), Pharaoh's army (Exod. 14), Gehazi's leprosy (2 Kings 5). His faithfulness and truth are glorified by miracles performed in fulfillment of his covenant promises, such as Sarah's conception (Gen. 21). All of God's works, whether normal or miraculous, are ordained to manifest his glory. This is the clear witness of the Old Testament regarding the purpose of miracles. And it plays an important part in helping us understand why miracles take place.

3

Why Did
Miracles Occur
in the Ministry of Christ

?

Jesus Christ was the greatest miracle worker the world has ever seen. His ministry was a constant exhibition of the love and power of God. His miracles were of every conceivable kind. Through them he showed his power over the physical world (Matt. 14:13–33; 21:18–22; Mark 4:35–41; Luke 5:1–11; John 2:1–11; 21:1–16), over the spirit world (Matt. 17:14–21; Mark 1:21–28; 5:1–20), and over sickness (Matt. 12:9–13; Mark 9:25; Luke 13:10–17; John 4:43–54).

There was no sickness that Christ could not heal. He gave sight to the blind (Matt. 9:27–31; Mark 10:46–52). He healed the most despised sickness of the Jews, leprosy (Mark 1:40–45; Luke 17:11–19). He even raised the dead (Matt. 9:18–26; Luke 7:11–16; John 11:1–46). His healing touch at times reached the sick in distant cities (Matt. 8:5–13; John 4:43–54). He even healed his enemies (Matt. 26:51–56). The kind and powerful works of Jesus were so abundant that John ended his Gospel with these words: "And there are also many other things which Jesus did, the which, if they should be written every one, I suppose that even the world itself could not contain the books that should be written" (John 21:25).

The authenticity of Christianity is inseparable from the reality of Christ's miracles. If the miracles did not happen, our faith is a hoax. The Gospel writers mention names, places and times that would have made the verification of their claims rather easy. Any skeptical person could have investigated these miracles for himself. They were obvious and indisputable. This is all true of the greatest miracle, also, the resurrection of Christ. By this single miracle Christ was "declared to be the Son of God with power" (Rom. 1:4). Paul argued that if Christ did not rise from the dead, then our faith was in vain and all the apostles were deceivers (1 Cor. 15:14, 15).

Luke was not overstating the case when he declared that Christ "shewed himself alive after his passion by many infallible proofs, being seen of them forty days" (Acts 1:3). Paul reminded King Agrippa of the powerful evidence in support of the resurrection, saying, "For the king knoweth of these things, before whom also I speak freely: for I am persuaded that none of these things are hidden from him; for this thing was not done in a corner" (Acts 26:26). Paul catalogues six different public appearances of Jesus after his resurrection, and this was only a partial list (1 Cor. 15:4–8). These men were not hesitant to advance the evidence in support of the miracles of the New Testament.

Why did Jesus perform miracles? The primary reason was to glorify God. The power and mercy of God were exalted every time he healed the sick. When Jesus was told of the advanced sickness of Lazarus, he replied, "This sickness is not unto death, but for the glory of God, that the Son of God might be glorified thereby" (John 11:4; also 9:1–3). The character of God fully shone through Jesus. He was "the brightness of his [God's] glory and the express image of his person" (Heb. 1:3). To have seen Jesus, then, was to have beheld God. Jesus was God incarnate, in the flesh. How would God act if he were on earth? That question was forever answered by the life of Christ. To have seen him was to have seen the Father. To reject him is to reject the clearest revelation of God ever made to man. John affirmed, "No man hath seen God at any time; the only begotten Son, which is in the bosom of the Father, he hath declared him" (John 1:18).

Many times we read of Jesus being touched by the needs of those around him. He responded to these needs by expressing his love and sympathy through kind words and miraculous healing power. This is remembered by Peter in his description of Christ as One "who went about doing good, and healing all that were oppressed of the devil; for God was with him" (Acts 10:38). Another design of his miracles, then, was to show God's concern for the needs of his sinful, helpless creatures.

Miracles also served to authenticate him as the Messiah, the Son of God. When the Jews asked him if he were the Messiah, he replied, "I told you, and ye believed not: the works that I do in my Father's name, they bear witness of me" (John 10:25; also 3:2; 6:14; 20:30, 31). Christ's miracles attested to his deity. Jesus was "a man approved of God among you by miracles and wonders and signs, which God did by him in the midst of you, as ye yourselves also know" (Acts 2:22). Miracles adorned the life of Jesus because he was the sinless Son of God, sent into the world to reveal the love and grace of God to sinners. He said, "But I have greater witness than that of John: for the works which the Father hath given me to finish, the same works that I do, bear witness of me, that the Father hath sent me" (John 5:36).

Miracles were also performed and recorded to assist people to believe on Christ. John declared, "And many other signs truly did Jesus in the presence of his disciples, which are not written in this book: but these are written, that ye might believe that Jesus is the Christ, the Son of God; and that believing ye might have life through his name" (John 20:30, 31). The resurrection of Lazarus had a profound spiritual effect on the hearts of many. John states, "Then many of the Jews which came to Mary, and had seen the things which Jesus did, believed on him" (John 11:45). Even the Pharisees wondered, "What do we? for this man doeth many miracles. If we let him thus alone, all men will believe on him." (John 11:47, 48).

Commenting on John 20:30, 31, Calvin wrote:

> No other use is here assigned to miracles than to be the aids and supports of faith; for they serve to prepare the minds of men, that they may cherish greater reverence for the word of God, and we know how cold and sluggish our attention is, if we be not excited by something else. . . . Although, therefore, strictly speaking, faith rests on the word of God, and looks to the word as its only end, still the addition of miracles is not superfluous, provided that they be also viewed as relating to the word, and direct faith towards it (Calvin 1984, 18:A:281).

John Calvin made an important point when he united the gracious design of miracles with the Word of God. Miracles, apart from revelation, are not sanctifying. They are not automatic channels for the conveyance of blessing. The history of the Israelites in the wilderness is a perfect illustration of this. They were miraculously delivered from Egypt, but almost immediately lapsed into idolatry at the foot of Mt. Sinai. Soon after receiving God's law, they complained and were miraculously fed with manna. Nevertheless, they continued to complain. Miracles can lead to judgment instead of blessing, if not sanctified to the hearts of God's people by the Spirit of God.

Jesus spoke of a similar illustration in the remarkable story of the rich man and Lazarus in Luke 16. We will pick up the story where the rich man is beseeching Abraham:

> I pray thee therefore, father, that thou wouldest send him to my father's house: for I have five brethren; that he may testify unto them, lest they also come into this place of torment. Abraham saith unto him, They have Moses and the prophets; let them hear them. And he said, Nay, father Abraham: but if one

went unto them from the dead, they will repent. And he said unto them, If they hear not Moses and the prophets, neither will they be persuaded, though one rose from the dead (Luke 16:27–31).

This narrative strikingly asserts that miracles, apart from the teaching of God's Word, have no spiritual benefit. The main issue should not be the exhibition of miracles, but the proclamation of the whole counsel of God. We can be saved without observing miracles; but we cannot be saved apart from the Word of God (1 Peter 1:23; Rom. 10:13–15).

The Bible is clear, then, in relating the purpose of miracles as follows:

1. They were powerful tools through which God was glorified and his nature revealed.
2. They authenticated certain men as God's inspired messengers to mankind.
3. They prepared people to believe the Word.
4. They confirmed the faith of those who had already believed.
5. They specially revealed the deep love and concern that God has for his needy creatures.
6. They manifested the undeniable fact that Jesus was God in the flesh, the promised Messiah, sent to destroy the kingdom of Satan and to bring everlasting righteousness.

Miracles Today?

The divine purpose in working miracles has been revealed in the statements of Scripture. If miracles wrought by God's power occur in our day, they will have the same purpose as those that occurred in Bible times. I firmly believe that God does work miracles today. We have an omnipotent God; but there are two things he will not do.

First, God can never work against his own nature. He is unchangeable. If he worked against his nature, he would cease to be God, for he would change. The omnipotent and omniscient Lord cannot be the source behind a miracle manifesting weakness, incompleteness, or confusion.

Secondly, he will never oppose his Word. He honors his Word even in greater ways than he honors his own name (Ps. 138:2). The things he has revealed to us in his Word belong to us and to our children forever (Deut. 29:29). The Word of God is forever settled in heaven (Ps. 119:89; also 119:152, 160). The Spirit of God is represented as always working with and never against the Word of God (Eph. 6:17). Miracles directly from God never support error. If there is nothing stated in God's Word which declares that he will not work miracles in our day, we must assume that he can. Walter Chantry correctly affirms:

> And there is no Biblical reason to limit God to performing miracles at certain seasons only. No doubt God is yet executing unusual feats of power. In response to the prayers of his people, God is healing in sovereign power some whom modern medicine has pronounced hopeless. . . . God's working of wonders cannot be limited to ages past (Chantry 1979, 8).

One significant difference, though, between our days and those of the Bible concerns prophets. I agree with the many who affirm that God is no longer giving inspired messages to his people through unique spokesmen (see Appendix 1, "Is the Bible an Open System?"). One of the chief functions of miracles was to authenticate God's prophets. When we take away the need to verify God's messengers by miracles today, a significant purpose for the occurrence of miracles is removed. It is evident why miracles should abound in days when God was proclaiming new revelation to mankind. In a day, however, without new revelation, miracles should not be expected to be as profuse.

John Calvin spoke of this fact when he wrote:

> In demanding miracles from us, they [Romanists] act dishonestly; for we have not coined some new gospel, but retain the very one the truth of which is confirmed by all the miracles which Christ and the apostles ever wrought (Calvin 1979, 8).

Those who claim to speak new revelations from God must substantiate their claim by miracles. But those of us who follow only the Bible are contented that its miracles have more than sufficiently substantiated its truth. And if the Lord sees fit to magnify himself by some miracle united to our lives and ministries, perhaps in answer to our prayers or in direct confrontation with Satan's kingdom, we must humbly deflect all the honor to Christ, declaring, "Thine is the kingdom and the power and the glory forever. Amen."

4

Do Miraculous Gifts Exist Today

?

One of the hottest debates engaging the ranks of Evangelicalism is whether or not supernatural gifts are permanent gifts of God to the church. This is probably the single most important topic in our book. We will carefully develop our answer to this important question over the next four chapters. This chapter will introduce the topic.

Let us focus carefully on the question asked in the title of this chapter. The question is not, Do miracles occur today? Our God is an omnipotent God. He is a miracle-working God. He does occasionally work miracles in our day. But there is a difference between miracles and miraculous gifts. When Peter raised Dorcas from the dead, a great miracle occurred (Acts 9:36–42). But nowhere is raising the dead enumerated as one of the gifts of the Holy Spirit. This is an important distinction. Thus, one can believe that God works miracles of healing and deliverance without believing that miraculous gifts function today. I do not believe that the supernatural gifts of the Holy

Spirit exist today. I want you to know exactly why this is my conviction.

One of the most popular defenders of the supernatural gift position is John Wimber. He is the founder of the fast-growing group called the Vineyard Christian Fellowship. The distinctive features of the VCF are carefully portrayed by Wimber in his two popular works *Power Evangelism* (1986) and *Power Healing* (1987). His chief distinction is power evangelism. He explains:

> Once I accepted the fact that all the spiritual gifts are for today, I found a key for effective evangelism: combining the proclamation with the demonstration of gospel. . . . There is unusual power and effectiveness in this form of evangelism, which is the reason that I call it "power evangelism" (Wimber 1986, xx).

The underlying principle of power evangelism is the assumption that the supernatural gifts should function in the church today. Why do so many disagree with this belief? Wimber explains:

> Many evangelicals sincerely think that only Scripture study forms their thinking on such issues as healing or power evangelism. They are unaware of how powerful the influences of a Western, materialistic worldview are, how that worldview affects their perception of the supernatural in Scripture (Wimber 1986, 82).

He believes that Western Christians oppose the miraculous gifts because they have been subtly influenced by their materialistic world view. I think that he has a definite point. I agree that secularism has infiltrated and crippled large sections of the church in the West. There are thousands who think that their doctrinal position is the result of Bible study; but, in fact, it is simply warmed-over Rationalism. The supernatural to them is both irrelevant and unrealistic. They do not see themselves as living in the world of the Bible, a world where God is at work and of which angels and demons are a very real part.

This, however, is not what keeps me from endorsing miraculous gifts in our day. I believe in a miracle-working God. I believe that true signs, wonders, and mighty deeds are occurring in our day. The devil and his evil host are as real to me as my next door neighbors. I am not a materialist. This is not why I disagree with John Wimber and his companions. The following illustration highlights the chief difference I have with Pastor Wimber.

B. B. Warfield was a devout theologian of the old Princeton Seminary. He was one of the finest biblical scholars of his day. He bravely defended the entire Christian faith against the many scholars who were denying it. Warfield particularly championed the doctrine of the divine inspiration of the Bible. He loved the Bible and studied it with a thoroughness and understanding rarely paralleled by Christians of any age. His studies on the theme of miracles are very helpful.

Warfield taught that the miraculous gifts of the Holy Spirit were not intended as permanent gifts of God to the church. He was not the originator of this view. This has been the position of the church down through the ages. In the next chapter I will show the scriptural basis for this view.

Wimber dismisses the teaching of Dr. Warfield as follows: "No Scripture passage either states or implies his position" (Wimber 1986, 119). This is a rather bold and remarkable claim. With one simple statement John Wimber disclaims the belief held by the vast majority of Christians down through the ages and so well-stated by Warfield. Certainly, if John Wimber is right, then no Christian should accept Warfield's position for a minute. But if Wimber is wrong, then he has most unfairly impugned the testimony of a man who selflessly labored in defense of the faith. And I simply believe that John Wimber is wrong in accusing Warfield of espousing an unbiblical perspective concerning miraculous gifts.

The basic reason why I disagree with John Wimber, then, is not that we share different world views. Our view of life and reality is based upon God's inspired revelation, the Bible. Our difference in this area is simply that we disagree over the teaching of the Bible on the theme of miracles. I will show in the next chapter a very important fact concerning miracles that is totally ignored by Wimber. Jesus instructs us to "search the Scriptures" (John 5:39). We do this, humbly depending on the Holy Spirit to lead us into all truth. We must not become enslaved by any doctrine or experience inconsistent with its infallible teaching.

Several questions immediately arise as relevant to settling this issue. How were miraculous gifts conferred in the New Testament? Do the miraculous gifts mentioned in the New Testament correspond to their alleged counterparts in Christian experience today? When someone today claims to have the gift of tongues or the gift of healing, does the person's experience match those of the New Testament Christians who possessed the gifts? All these questions can be answered with certainty. And if they are answered with finality, then we have answered the entire question about the permanence of miraculous gifts.

5

How Were Miraculous Gifts Conferred upon New Testament Believers

?

Jesus conferred miracle-working power on his disciples when he sent them through Palestine. "And when he had called unto him his twelve disciples, he gave them power against unclean spirits, to cast them out, and to heal all manner of sickness" (Matt. 10:1; Luke 10:17—20). Every miracle they performed, then, could be traced back to Jesus as the source. The Lord Jesus said, "He that receiveth you receiveth me" (Matt. 10:40). It was he who was working through them.

During Christ's life on earth we see no other person conferring such power on another. The disciples are nowhere portrayed as granting others the power that they enjoyed. It is evident, also, that the miracle-working power they possessed was not given to them permanently. It was theirs only when they were fulfilling a mission on which Jesus had sent them. After his ascension, the apostles were not to begin immediately their ministries. They were told, "Tarry ye in the city of

Jerusalem, until ye be endued with power from on high" (Luke 24:49).

The first instance of the outpouring of the miraculous gifts of the Holy Spirit was on the day of Pentecost. That was a unique experience in the life of the church simply because it was the beginning of the Spirit's new work. Beginnings happen once. Pentecost has not occurred again, nor ever will. The reason for this is simple. Having filled the apostles with the Holy Spirit, the Lord then chose them to be his channels of power. They were to be specially used by God to supervise the growth of Christianity from its center in Jerusalem "unto the uttermost part of the earth" (Acts 1:8). They were the foundation of the church, with Jesus Christ being the chief cornerstone (Eph. 2:20; 1 Cor. 12:28, 29). Foundations are laid only once.

After the apostles received the power of the Spirit, the norm was established. They played a unique role of leadership in the spiritual and physical development of the New Testament church. Jesus directed the church through them (Acts 1:1, 2). There is no account of the imparting of miraculous gifts except through the ministry of an apostle of Jesus Christ. This could not be more clearly stated than it is in Acts 8:5–19.

The Samaritan Christians

Then Philip went down to the city of Samaria, and preached Christ unto them. And the people with one accord gave heed unto those things which Philip spake, hearing and seeing the miracles which he did. For unclean spirits, crying with loud voice, came out of many that were possessed with them: and many taken with palsies, and that were lame, were healed. And there was great joy in that city. But there was a certain man, called Simon, which beforetime in the same city used sorcery, and bewitched the people of Samaria, giving out that himself was some great one: to whom they all gave heed, from the least to the greatest, saying, This man is the great power of God. And to him they had regard, because that of long time he had bewitched them with sorceries. But when they believed Philip preaching the things concerning the kingdom of God, and the name of Jesus Christ, they were baptized, both men and women. Then Simon himself believed also: and when he was baptized, he continued with Philip, and wondered, beholding the miracles and signs which were done.

Now when the apostles which were at Jerusalem heard that Samaria had received the word of God, they sent unto them Peter and John: who, when they were come down, prayed for them, that they might receive the Holy Ghost: (For as yet he was fallen upon none of them: only they were baptized in the name of the Lord Jesus.) Then laid they their hands on them, and they received the Holy Ghost. And when Simon saw that through laying on of the apostles' hands the Holy Ghost was given, he offered them money, saying, Give me also this power, that on whomsoever I lay hands, he may receive the Holy Ghost (Acts 8:5–19).

The first Princeton Seminary professor, Archibald Alexander (1772–1851), gives a recounting of this occurrence as follows:

When the apostles at Jerusalem heard of the great success of the gospel at Samaria, they deputed two of their number to visit the place; particularly for the purpose of communicating the miraculous gifts of the Holy Ghost, which were at that time bestowed on the churches; but which were only given by the laying on of the hands of the apostles. When Simon saw that through the laying on of the hands of the apostles, the miraculous gifts of the Holy Ghost were given, he thought within himself, what he might accomplish, if possessed of such power as that exercised by Peter and John (A. Alexander 1850, 481, 482).

Luke was a careful historian. He outlined the propagation of the gospel from Jerusalem at every significant step. The Samaritans had already been converted and baptized by the time of the apostles' arrival. The Spirit had already been bestowed in his regenerating presence, or else they could not have believed (see Rom. 8:9; Acts 16:14). But the visible, miracle-working presence of the Spirit was lacking. When the apostles laid their hands on the Samaritan believers, the supernatural gifts of the Holy Spirit were bestowed. They were seen by Simon, so they were outward miracles.

Philip was a miracle worker (Acts 8:7, 13). So why could he not confer these like signs upon the Samaritans through prayer in Jesus' name? The simple and obvious answer is: Philip was not an apostle. Philip could preach and perform miracles; but it was God's will that only the apostles could bestow miraculous gifts.

Warfield concludes:

> It could not be more emphatically stated that the Holy Ghost was conferred by the laying on of the hands, specifically of the Apostles, and of the Apostles alone; what Simon is said to have seen is precisely that it was through the laying on of the hands of just the Apostles that the Holy Ghost was given. And there can be no question that it was specifically the extraordinary gifts of the Spirit that were in discussion. . . . (Warfield 1972, 22).

The First Gentile Christians

There are other texts that imply the same truth. Through the ministry of the apostle Peter, miraculous gifts were imparted by the Lord unto the first Gentile converts, Cornelius and his associates. Luke records:

> While Peter yet spake these words, the Holy Ghost fell on all them which heard the word. And they of the circumcision which believed were astonished, as many as came with Peter, because that on the Gentiles also was poured out the gift of the Holy Ghost. For they heard them speak with tongues, and mag-nify God (Acts 10:44–46).

The Ephesian Christians

The connection between the apostles and the miraculous gifts is apparent in Paul's ministry, too. He came across some of John the Baptist's disciples in Ephesus. Luke states:

Then said Paul, John verily baptized with the baptism of repentance, saying unto the people that they should believe on him which should come after him, that is, on Christ Jesus. When they heard this, they were baptized in the name of the Lord Jesus. And when Paul had laid his hands upon them, the Holy Ghost came on them; and they spake with tongues, and prophesied (Acts 19:4–6).

Luke constantly makes a note of the sign gifts being conferred through the apostles' ministries, because it was a unique feature of an apostle. This ability was one of the "signs of an apostle." The signs of an apostle were those unique aspects of his life and ministry that authenticated him as one of Christ's representatives. Through the presence of these signs, people would be able to distinguish between true and false apostles.

The Corinthian Christians

Paul's ministry in Corinth was undermined by "false apostles" who were preaching "another Jesus" (2 Cor. 11:3–6, 13–15). They were causing the Corinthian Christians to doubt Paul's apostolicity. Paul authenticated his divine call by reminding the Corinthians: "Truly the signs of an apostle were wrought among you in all patience, in signs, and wonders, and mighty deeds" (2 Cor. 12:12). It was through Paul that the Corinthians had come to enjoy such a wide display of supernatural gifts.

The Roman Christians

The church at Rome was evidently not founded by an apostle. Although there is no definite word in Scripture concerning its origin, it probably was begun by those converted to Christianity while on a pilgrimage to Jerusalem. Acts 2:10 (ASV) records that there were "sojourners from Rome, both Jews and

proselytes" present in Jerusalem on the celebrated day of Pentecost when the Holy Spirit came down. It is specifically mentioned that some of these Romans heard the first speaking in
tongues. It is highly probable that some were saved and discipled in the faith in Jerusalem, eventually returning to their
homeland.

The apostle Paul wanted to visit the Roman Christians. He
wrote, "For I long to see you, that I may impart unto you some
spiritual gift, to the end ye may be established" (Rom. 1:11).
The Romans apparently had not enjoyed the benefits of an
apostolic ministry. Paul wanted them to realize that great
things would occur when he visited them. He stated:

> For I will not dare to speak of any of those things which
> Christ hath not wrought by me, to make the Gentiles obedient,
> by word and deed, through mighty signs and wonders, by the
> power of the Spirit of God; so that from Jerusalem, and round
> about unto Illyricum, I have fully preached the gospel of
> Christ. . . . For which cause also I have been much hindered
> from coming to you. . . . And I am sure that, when I come unto
> you, I shall come in the fulness of the blessing of the gospel of
> Christ (Rom. 15:18, 19, 22, 29).

The only miraculous gift mentioned in Romans as being
practiced by Christians of that city was the gift of prophecy
(Rom. 12:6–8). This could have been conferred by the apostles
on the Roman leaders while they were still in Jerusalem,
shortly after their conversion to Christianity. It is interesting
that the list of gifts in 1 Corinthians 12:7–10 mentions some
nine miraculous gifts operative in Corinth. Paul longed for this
"fulness" to be experienced in Rome, also.

Timothy

Paul wrote to Timothy: "Wherefore I put thee in re-
membrance that thou stir up the gift of God, which is in thee
by the putting on of my hands" (2 Tim. 1:6). There is disagreement among the commentators whether this is referring to a

miraculous gift or to ordination (see 1 Tim. 4:14). Nevertheless, the mentioning of a gift together with the laying on of an apostle's hands again gives important biblical evidence that gifts and the apostolic ministry were vitally connected.

Both the direct statements and the implications of the Scriptures support the teaching that miraculous gifts were bestowed only through the agency of an apostle. The conclusion, then, is that when the apostles ceased living, the miraculous gifts ceased being conferred. The one was dependent upon the other. If the office of an apostle was limited to a specific time, then the era of miraculous gifts was also limited. We would expect to find that as years elapsed, the original apostles would all die, and as a natural result, miraculous gifts would decline proportionately. Although they would outlive the apostles for a while, supernatural gifts would eventually be terminated with the death of the last Christian to whom they were conferred through an apostle.

Admittedly, this chapter proves nothing if there are apostles in every age. But, if it can be proven that apostles existed only temporarily in the church's history, then it is proven with certainty that those supernatural gifts that depend on them for their existence must also have been temporary. Therefore, we must now investigate what Scripture says about the office of an apostle.

6

Are There
Apostles Today

?

I have frequently asked Bible-college graduates if they could tell me the signs of an apostle. Usually I get blank stares in return, as if I have asked some deep metaphysical question. Few students are being taught the distinguishing marks of the apostolic office; the unique role played by the apostles is unappreciated. This is one of those key bits of information that has fallen through the cracks of today's Christian education. The result of this oversight has been catastrophic.

It is impossible to understand the miraculous gifts of the New Testament without understanding their relationship to the apostles of Jesus Christ. We cannot correctly apply any biblical doctrine if we are ignorant of the historical, biblical context that defines that doctrine. We would rightly question the credentials of one who teaches that a person is saved by good works. If someone has not read and assimilated the teaching of Scripture on salvation, how can that person teach others what they must do to be saved? That message might be entertaining, but it is only as true as it is biblical. So is the case of the person who teaches on the subject of miraculous gifts without understanding the doctrine of miracles as it is declared in the Word of God. It might be an entertaining and even compelling message. But if it is built on a foundation other than the Word of God, the edifice will not endure. Let us, then, look carefully at the office of an apostle.

The Title of the Office

The word *apostle* is used some eighty times in the New Testament. A study of these texts clearly reveals its meaning. In each case this term identifies an individual who had been delegated with full authority to represent another. An apostle is a commissioned agent, an ambassador, performing an act in the name of the one who sent him. It is always in this sense that the word is used in the New Testament.

Primary Meaning

The word *apostle* is primarily used for those men specifically chosen and delegated by Christ to be his witnesses. Their number was originally twelve (Matt. 10:2–4; Luke 6:13–16). Judas Iscariot was replaced by Matthias (Acts 1:15–26), a decision nowhere opposed in Scripture, and powerfully defended by J. Addison Alexander (1809–1860) in his commentary on Acts (see J. A. Alexander 1980a, 37, 38).

The number of Christ's apostles broadened somewhat from the Twelve according to 1 Corinthians 15:5–8. Paul was commissioned as "the apostle of the Gentiles" (Acts 9:15; Gal. 1:16; 2:7–9; Rom. 11:13). James, the brother of the Lord, received a personal commission from Christ (1 Cor. 15:7) and was declared an apostle (Gal. 1:19). So there may have been other apostles, such as Barnabas (Acts 14:4, 14), whose personal histories are not as well known. The qualifications for this position were of such a nature, though, that their number could not have been many, as we shall see.

Secondary Meaning

There was a more general use of the word *apostle* in New Testament times. Jesus, of course, was not the only person to have delegated representatives. Hence, whenever we find such agents, we should not be surprised to find them termed apostles. If a congregation commissioned an individual for a specific duty, he was designated their apostle. (See 2 Cor. 8:23 and Phil. 2:25 where *messenger* is the Greek word *apostle*.) So, Epaphroditus was the Philippians' apostle. He was officially sent by the church to the imprisoned Paul.

A very real danger arises when there is no distinction made between the primary and secondary usages of this term. Though we are all sent to witness, none of us have the prerogatives of Christ's chosen representatives. Some today are claiming equal status with Christ's apostles. They claim divine inspiration and demand total obedience. Unfortunately, they often have followers who will submit to them. This usurpation of the apostolic office is both unfortunate and unnecessary. An objective study of the nature of the apostolic office will assuredly lead us to the conclusion that it cannot be a permanent office in the church.

The Nature of the Office

It is precisely at this point where many Christians are in such need of biblical instruction. Counterfeit bills are most effective among those who have not studied what the original looks like. Likewise, when Christians forget the distinguishing marks of a true apostle, it is much more likely that they will be fooled by a false apostle. What, then, are the signs of an apostle? The importance of rightly answering this question is highlighted in the following statement by one of America's greatest theologian, Charles Hodge (1797–1878):

> The signs of an apostle were the insignia of the apostleship; those things which by divine appointment were made the evidence of a mission from God. When these were present an obligation rested on all who witnessed them to acknowledge the

authority of those who bore those insignia. When they were absent, it was, on the one hand, an act of sacrilege to claim the apostleship; and, on the other, an act of apostasy from God to admit its possession. To acknowledge the claims of those who said they were apostles and were not, was (and is) to turn from God to the creature, to receive as divine what was in fact human or Satanic (C. Hodge n.d., 290, 291).

A man was an apostle of Jesus Christ only if the following were true in his life:

1. He must have been an eyewitness of the resurrection of Jesus Christ. He personally saw the risen Christ (Acts 1:21–23; 1 Cor. 9:1).
2. He must have been personally taught divine truth (the gospel) by Jesus Christ (Gal. 1:11, 12; 1 Cor. 15:3).
3. He received the gift of divine inspiration, or that influence of the Holy Spirit that made him errorless in the communication of the Word (John 14:26; 16:13; 1 Cor. 2:10–13; 14:37; 1 Thess. 2:13; 1 John 4:6).
4. He had the power of working various types of miracles in confirming his mission (2 Cor. 12:12; Rom. 15:18, 19; Heb. 2:4; Acts 5:12; 14:3).
5. He had the ability to confer miraculous gifts on others (Acts 8:18; 19:6).
6. He could speak forth words of judgment in the name of the Lord and have them miraculously executed (John 20:23; Acts 5:3–11; 13:10, 11; 1 Cor. 5:3–5; 1 Tim. 1:20).
7. He exercised a position of authority over local churches and pastors, demanding obedience and compliance (1 Cor. 5:3–5; 2 Cor. 10:6, 8, 11; 2 Thess. 3:14; Phil. 3–17, 18; 2 Thess. 3:7–12).
8. He taught nothing contradictory to the Word of God (Gal. 1:8, 9).
9. His preaching of the Word was with great power and fruitfulness (John 15:16; 1 Cor. 9:2; 2 Cor. 3:2, 3; 1 Thess. 1:5).

10. His life was one of holiness, humility, self-discipline, and selfless dedication (1 Cor. 9:16–22; 2 Cor. 6:1–10; 11:22–33; 1 Peter 5:1–4; 1 John 1:1–7).

Who today claims to possess all the above credentials? Only if they do are they worthy of the name *apostle*. The very nature of these qualifications precludes them from being realized in our day. What living person has physically seen the Lord and been commissioned as his witness? The office of apostle is incapable of permanence within the church. Those who claim to possess it without exhibiting its characteristics are deceived. And those who follow them do so to their own destruction.

The church is "built upon the foundation of the apostles and prophets" (Eph. 2:20). The church is here likened to a spiritual building raised up on them, with Jesus Christ "being the chief cornerstone." The groundbreaking work of the apostles is a matter of history. They were the first Christians, the pro-claimers of true doctrine, verified by miraculous gifts, planters of the church throughout the world, and the authors of the New Testament. They performed unique services, and hence were uniquely qualified. To claim that apostles live and exert their authority in our day is to attempt to rebuild the church, to re-lay the foundation that has been once and forever established. It is an effort that instead of building the church may damage it irreparably.

Two significant points have been firmly established in the last two chapters. First, miraculous gifts were conferred on New Testament Christians through the agency of an apostle of Jesus Christ. Secondly, it is impossible for apostles to exist today. There are none living who possess the necessary credentials of an apostle.

The question, Do miraculous gifts exist today? therefore has been answered. Because miraculous gifts were inextricably bound to the ministry of the apostles, they could not endure beyond the lives of those directly influenced by the apostles.

But some will argue from their own experience, "We have the gifts functioning in our own lives!" Well, if this is true, then I must be wrong. The following chapter will compare the alleged miraculous gifts of our day with the real supernatural gifts of the Spirit as seen in the New Testament.

Probing
Contemporary Claims
and Their Sources

7

Does Anyone Have the Gift of Healing Today

?

No topic could arouse more feeling than that of healing. The desire to see the sick healed is a universal human emotion. Our hearts are deeply touched when we view another human being suffering from disease. It is a most natural Christian act, then, to pray in behalf of the sick. And we are all filled with joy when God answers such prayers by mercifully healing the one in need.

There are some, though, who take this natural concern for the sick a step further. The power of prayer does not always produce healing, so they seek greater power. Some assert that greater power is theirs because the Lord has given to them the gift of healing. That is, they have received a miraculous gift from God whereby they are called to serve the church by healing the sick in Jesus' name. What a glorious thing it would be if there were servants of God possessing such healing power. Does anyone in fact possess such a gift?

The gift of healing is mentioned in 1 Corinthians 12:9, 28, and 30, but it is not defined in those texts. We are certain that any gift which manifests the supernatural power of God will not fail. Failure to accomplish our own will arises from either a lack of power or wisdom, but the omnipotent Spirit of God has no such deficiency. The gift of healing is confirmed, then, by the ability to completely heal a person in the name of Jesus.

The gift of healing is clearly seen in the ministries of Christ and his apostles. When we compare the healing ministries of today with Christ's and his apostles', we are struck with the many evident differences.

There are some modern-day "healers" who have been exposed as fakes, such as Peter Popoff. Some have become wealthy through this sort of evil trickery. Many people, therefore, have declared that all such ministries are evil counterfeits. But this approach to the issue is far too simplistic. The issue is not so easily resolved. You see, there are others, such as C. Peter Wagner and John Wimber, who refuse to charge anything for their healing ministry. They take very seriously the command of Jesus, "Freely ye have received, freely give" (Matt. 10:8). So not everyone in this line of work is a money-hungry charlatan.

Our purpose in this chapter is to look at the gift as it functioned in the New Testament and compare it with the ministries of those claiming to have the same gift today. Many of them quote the Scriptures and claim they have the same gift of healing enjoyed by New Testament believers. They declare that the Holy Spirit generates the gift in them as he did in the apostles.

Whether these claims are true or false is a matter for objective comparison. There is no reason for us to be confused, for God does not change. They are the same gifts as those of the New Testament only if they share the same characteristics. This is the only way to prove whether or not the gift exists today. We cannot simply take the word of an individual, who may sincerely believe that he or she has the gift, yet be wrong. If it is the same gift that was possessed by Christ and his apostles, then the evidences today will be identical with those seen in the earlier healing ministries.

The Healing Ministry of Christ

The following points reveal the characteristics of Christ's healing ministry:

1. Christ did not require faith of everyone before healing them.

> The centurion's servant (Matt. 8:5–10). The faith shown here was that of the centurion, not of the man healed.
>
> The daughter of Jairus (Mark 5:35–43). The faith evidenced, again, was not that of the sick girl, but of her father.
>
> The demonized Gadarene (Luke 8:26–39). He was healed before he was capable of expressing faith.
>
> The ten lepers (Luke 17:11–19). All ten were healed, but only one possessed true, saving faith.
>
> Malchus (Luke 22:50, 51; John 18:10). One of those attempting to seize Jesus was healed after Peter cut his ear off.

Here is the great escape for many "faith healers": if people are not healed, it is because of their lack of faith, not because of any lack in the healer. But this is not healing power as Jesus possessed it. Some today argue that Jesus rewarded the faith of individuals by healing them, for he often said, "Thy faith hath made thee whole" (Mark 5:34; 10:52, etc.). This is true, but it is not equivalent to demanding faith of everyone. He would not punish those who had no faith and he would not withhold healing from them. But he did not demand faith of everyone he healed. The following quotation is a typical example of the popular but erroneous demand for faith prior to healing:

Those who receive must believe for the benefits. As no sinner can be saved until he believes it is God's Will to save him and until he receives by faith, so no sick person can be healed until he believes it is God's Will to heal him and until he receives the benefits by faith. Scriptures . . . show how Jesus healed only those who believed for healing (Jorstadt 1973, 105).

The pain and anguish that this position produces is well described by Dr. William Nolen, a medical doctor who extensively investigated the healing ministry of Kathryn Kuhlman:

As I stood in the corridor watching the hopeless cases leave, seeing the tears of the parents as they pushed their crippled children to the elevators, I wished Miss Kuhlman had been with me. . . . I wondered whether she sincerely felt that the joy of those "cured" of bursitis and arthritis compensated for the anguish of those left with their withered legs, their imbecilic children, their cancers of the liver (Nolen 1974, 60).

Certainly one's heart is burdened when it contemplates the enormous magnitude of disappointment and despair that accompanies these mass healing services. Can the same Holy Spirit that brought joy to the hundreds healed by Christ be the author of a "gift" that results in so much despair?

2. Christ healed all.

Over and over again this statement is made in the Gospels. "When the even was come, they brought unto him many that were possessed with devils: and he cast out the spirits with his word, and healed all that were sick" (Matt. 8:16). "But when Jesus knew it, he withdrew himself from thence: and great multitudes followed him, and he healed them all" (Matt. 12:15). See also Matt. 4:24; 9:35; 14:14 and Luke 4:40.

Jesus was not selective, but healed everyone presented to him. There is no instance of a sick person being brought to Jesus whom he did not heal. Indeed, when Peter summarized the ministry of Jesus, he emphasized this very point: "How God anointed Jesus of Nazareth with the Holy Ghost and with power: who went about doing good, and healing all that were oppressed of the devil; for God was with him" (Acts 10:38).

How does this compare with the great failure of those claiming the gift of healing today? Most in healing ministries do not make known their rate of success. Dr. C. Peter Wagner is a refreshing exception in this way. He states: "71 percent of the people I have prayed for over the last two years are still sick to some degree after the prayer is over. Only 29 percent are completely healed" (Wagner 1988, 257). According to Wagner, the eighty prayer-and-healing teams in Wimber's Anaheim Vineyard Christian Fellowship keep careful records. In 1987 they recorded 26 percent became "completely well" through their healing ministry (Wagner, 1988, 244). It is wonderful that some are being healed. But is it not dangerous to claim to possess a "gift of the Holy Spirit" when, in fact, the "gift" evinces failure and imperfection? It is inconceivable to me that two utterly different things can be called the same. That which always succeeds is not the same as that which usually fails.

3. Christ healed all types of disease.

Organic disorders. These types of disease occur when an organ is destroyed or so injured that it cannot possibly function. Jesus healed the blind, the deaf, the severely crippled, diseases resulting from organs being beyond normal repair. Thus, it was an obvious miracle, something that produced wonder, when he healed such people. Although there are only isolated claims for this type of healing today, when such a claim is verified, what does it prove? Simply that God works miracles. It does not prove that a person has some functional gift of healing. A gift is a God-given ability that can normally function in an individual. A gift is not something that happens once a month, or 25 percent of the time.

Functional disorders. These occur when an organ is not functioning correctly. The organ itself is in good condition, but for one reason or another, its function is not occurring.

The mental, emotional, and spiritual conditions of individuals can affect the normal functioning of body organs. Physical sickness often occurs when there is some nonphysical disturbances. When the mental, emotional, or spiritual problem is solved, then the body functions normally again.

There were undoubtedly sick people in this condition healed by Christ. Matthew records, "And Jesus went about all the cities and villages, teaching in their synagogues, and preaching the gospel of the kingdom, and healing every sickness and every disease among the people" (Matt. 9:35). But those specific instances of healing recorded in the Gospels were mainly all types of organic diseases.

Some today claim the gift of healing, but proclaim that they have little or no success healing certain diseases. Wagner writes:

> Speaking of gifts, do not be surprised to find that some with the gift of healing have been given specialties in certain areas. Francis MacNutt, for example, has had little success in praying for deafness, but a fairly high degree of success in praying for bone problems and problems in the abdominal or chest area, except cancer. My specialty, as I have mentioned, is for lengthening legs (which in most cases involves pelvic adjustments) and problems relating to the spine (Wagner 1988, 215).

This is an unwarranted limiting of the gift of healing. It has no biblical parallel. Even within their area of specialization there is no one proving a 100 percent healing record.

Let us remember that the omnipotent Holy Spirit is the author of these gifts. Are we adding to his glory or detracting from it when we insist that we possess one of his gifts and manifest but little divine power in ministering it? I applaud Wagner and Wimber for their honesty. But this does not change the facts. He that professes to possess a gift without manifesting its characteristics is deceived. And deception is not of God.

Jesus often healed with a word or by a touch. He did not use theatrics or parade his gift before an audience. Instead, he often told the people not to advertise their healings (Matt. 8:4; Mark 7:36; Luke 8:56). He performed his miracles everywhere, not in some special setting where the atmosphere could be controlled. He needed no special props or conditions, because he was manifesting the mighty power of God. He worked healings while his enemies were watching. Everything was out in the open. It was evident to all people that Christ was from God. Nicodemus declared, "Rabbi, we know that thou art a teacher come from God: for no man can do these miracles that thou doest, except God be with him" (John 3:2).

Today's attempts fall immeasurably short of Christ's healing ministry. Yet, amazingly, most who assert the gift of healing is functioning today do so quoting John 14:12. In that verse Jesus said, "Verily, verily, I say unto you, He that believeth on me, the works that I do shall he do also; and greater works than these shall he do; because I go unto my Father." And today's "healers" dare to claim the fulfillment of this verse in themselves.

The Healing Ministry of the Apostles

Some today might try to evade comparison to Christ because he was God. Naturally, they would argue, Christ's healing ministry would be greater. But this does not explain their use of John 14:12. And neither does it explain the fact that all the points mentioned above concerning Christ were also true of his apostles.

The apostles did not demand faith of all they healed. Certainly, Dorcas did not have to exercise faith when Peter raised her from the dead (Acts 9:36–42). As Jesus did, the apostles healed everyone brought to them, as attested in Acts 5:16: "There came also a multitude out of the cities round about unto Jerusalem, bringing sick folks, and them which were vexed with unclean spirits: and they were healed every one." (See also Acts 28:9.)

The ability to heal was a gift of God to these men. The gift, though, was not to be abused. It was not given to assure its subject of perfect health or to favor his friends with the same. Jesus would miraculously feed five thousand, but he refused to use the same power to feed only himself (see Matt. 4:3–4; 14:13–21). Paul (2 Cor. 12:7–10), Timothy (1 Tim. 5:23), and Trophimus (2 Tim. 4:20) experienced sicknesses that were not divinely healed. God sometimes teaches us more by helping us endure sickness than by miraculously healing us.

Early in their training the apostles had to learn that spiritual gifts were not to be used as magic. They learned that the gifts were dependent upon the power of the Holy Spirit. If they attempted to use the gifts apart from the Spirit's guidance, in the humble spirit of prayer and utter dependence on God, they would fail (see Matt. 17:14–21; Luke 10:17–20). These believers evidently learned their lessons well. After Pentecost there is no instance of a person with the gift of healing ever failing when attempting to heal another person (see Acts 3:6–8; 8:6, 7; 14:8–10).

As Jesus did, they healed organic diseases. The apostles worked in the open. Indeed, their enemies were baffled when considering how to oppose them. They said, "What shall we do to these men? for that indeed a notable miracle hath been done by them is manifest to all them that dwell in Jerusalem; and we cannot deny it" (Acts 4:16). They healed totally and instantaneously (Acts 9:34). The power they evinced was the same as their Savior's. And indeed, this does not surprise us, because all their healings were performed in the name of Jesus Christ (Acts 3:12, 16).

What are we to think of those attempted healings today that fail? Is the name of Jesus less powerful today? Certainly not. The simple and candid fact is that the gift of healing no longer exists. Prayer for healing is to take place, as James 5:14, 15 teaches. God will sometimes bless with divine healing. Other times he graciously works through medicinal agents in healing the body. And often he gives us grace to bear the affliction for our good and his glory. This subject is further explored in appendix 2, "Is There Healing in the Atonement?"

The issue of healing need not be one of mystery and confusion. God does heal, but the gift of healing does not exist today. Those who are used of God in successfully praying for the healing of others ought not to exalt themselves by claiming the possession of a supernatural gift that they evidently do not possess. But neither should they stop praying for the sick. Those who "weep with them that weep" often will be led of God to pray for the healing of their sick friends and relatives. Compassion and mercy are godly attributes. The Spirit of God often seems to use those whose desires are most like his.

Satanic Counterfeits

I recognize that Satan's agents can heal. Such is declared in Scripture (Rev. 13:3, 4, 12). And it is also a fact of experience. Satan has been permitted by God to enact healings through many forms. Wagner notes:

> We see counterfeits in Haitian voodoo, in Brazilian spiritism, in African traditional religions, in the occult here in the United States and wherever witchcraft, magic and astrology are present. In Thailand, three-year-old "Dr. Noi" heals thousands with a magical tree bark. In India Hindus pierce their bodies with hooks and walk barefoot on live coals, feeling no pain (Wagner 1988, 245).

A former spiritualist medium, Raphael Gasson, declared:

> There are many, many Spiritualists today who are endowed with this remarkable gift of power by Satan, and I myself, having been used in this way, can testify to having witnessed miraculous healings taking place at "healing meetings" in Spiritualism (Gasson 1966, 109).

It should be understood that whenever a satanic healing

occurs, more is lost than is gained. Temporary alleviation of sickness or pain is exchanged for an increase of demonic influence within the person's life.

What About Other Gifts?

What is true of the gift of healing is true of the other supernatural gifts. An objective examination always reveals serious flaws in today's alleged gifts as compared with the biblical gifts. This is clearly evident regarding the gift of tongues. Much has been written on this subject already. The gift of tongues was the supernatural ability to speak in new languages as the situation arose. The context was usually evangelistic, as is evident from Acts 2. Wagner cites the example of one missionary who began to speak fluent Spanish (Wagner 1988, 158–159). Suppose this is true; what is proven? The gift mentioned in the New Testament (Acts 2:4; 10:46; 19:6; 1 Cor. 12:10, 30; 14:5, 18, 22) is constantly called the gift of tongues. Note that the word *tongues* is plural. It refers to a variety of languages, not to a single language. The gift was the miraculous ability to share the gospel in whatever language was needed at any given time. When Paul traveled through the interiors of different countries, he regularly met with new tribal languages and dialects. This posed no insurmountable problem to him, because he had the gift of tongues. As he testified, "I thank my God, I speak with tongues more than ye all" (1 Cor. 14:18).

I believe God can work miracles today. It does not stun me to hear of a missionary miraculously speaking a new language. If it is true, it is a miracle. It is not the gift of tongues. I can sincerely glorify God for such miracles. Our God is a merciful God. He takes no pleasure in the death of the wicked. There has never existed a human being who comes near to possessing the burden for the lost that fills our Savior and Lord. Hearing of miracles occurring today in verification of the further spread of the gospel message should not astound us.

Another alleged miraculous gift often mentioned is the

"word of knowledge." John Wimber speaks of these words as "promptings," "flashes of insight," or "mental pictures" (Wimber 1986, 53, 5, 62–3). He defines them as "a spiritual gift through which God reveals facts about a situation for which a person had no previous knowledge" (Wimber 1987, 240). But he also admits, "Over the years I have learned to recognize when these insights are from God and when they are a result of my imagination—or indigestion" (Wimber 1986, 62). Mistakes can and do occur. Does it take several years and many mistakes before anyone can distinguish a true word of knowledge from a presumption? I cannot believe that this is the gift mentioned by Paul in 1 Corinthians 12:8; 13:8. That which is directly from God manifests him clearly. There is far too much subjectivism in the alleged words of knowledge of most faith healers today. What objective tests are given to prove their accuracy? What penalty or discipline takes place when someone presumes to speak for the Lord and is wrong? Do we just say oops? If the gift occurs today, where is the individual who regularly receives insights from God of this miraculous nature, without mistakes interrupting the process? Being accurate part of the time is not good enough. "God is light, and in him is no darkness at all" (1 John 1:5).

I do not want to be misunderstood. The reader should not conclude that I have attacked Wimber's "flashes of insight" as demonic. He is wrong, I believe, in calling them the supernatural gift of "words of knowledge." But this does not mean they are of Satan. Wimber has led several people to professions of faith in Jesus Christ as a direct result of these spiritual "promptings." Is it possible that the Spirit of God can thus communicate information to use in leading hardened sinners to the Savior? I believe he can. And before you categorize me as a heretic, read the following quotations from revered Christian theologians whose orthodoxy is beyond question.

Archibald Alexander recounts the remarkable conversion of George Inglis, a wicked man who was inexplicably smitten with blindness. A godly woman offered to read him the Bible, which led to a great work of conviction in his soul. Following his conversion, Inglis is reported to have experienced a most remarkable "vision" which mightily confirmed his faith. Alexander states,

> What is here related is no doubt strictly true, but there is no propriety in calling it "a vision", since it can easily be accounted for by a vivid impression on the imagination. A vision is something supernatural seen with the bodily eyes; but this man was totally blind; the objects so clearly discerned must then have been from impressions on the imagination. But in saying this, it is not intended to deny that the cause was the Spirit of God. This divine Agent can and does produce vivid impressions on the imagination, which have so much the appearance of external realities, that many are persuaded that they do see and hear what takes place only in their own minds. (Alexander 1967, 91.)

The "impressions" of the Holy Spirit on Christians' minds mentioned by Alexander sounds very much like the "promptings" of John Wimber which God has used in drawing sinners to Christ. We must not reflexively condemn that which strikes us as odd or different. God is infinite; we are finite. If we "walk with God" in constant prayer should we not expect that he would intimately lead and guide us? This guidance by God's Spirit must be distinguished from God's inspired revelation which alone is the Christian's normative law for life. We certainly do not expect an audible voice because God can wonderfully lead our minds as we wait on him. Charles Hodge, when discussing the Christian's walk with God, stated,

> Communion cannot be one-sided. There must be conversation, address and answer. God does thus commune with us. He reveals himself to his people as he does not unto the world. He assures them of his love. He awakens in them confidence in his promises. He brings those promises to their minds, and gives them the power of response. These promises become his answers to their requests. And they experience a renewal of faith, love, zeal, etc., which is the manifestation of

his presence with the soul. This is not imaginary. It is real. It is not [fanaticism]. It does not suppose anything miraculous, no responses by voice, no unintelligent impulses; but the consciousness of the presence of the Infinite Spirit with our spirits; the conviction that he hears and answers us. We have probably all seen examples of this walking with God, men . . . who lived in habitual communion with God through Christ (C. Hodge, 1979, 254).

My statements, though, should not be construed as supporting every "healer" who declares a "word of knowledge" and mentions someone's hernia. Much guessing, presumption, and generalization is passed off as "words of knowledge." Nevertheless, when a lost soul is drawn to a saving knowledge of Jesus Christ through confrontation with a sensitive, Spirit-led Christian, we had better reserve passing judgment against them. God's elect will be saved. If the "orthodox" Christian does not sow in tears, he certainly will not reap in joy. And God will use those who are less "orthodox" and yet burdened for the lost in his great work of redemption. The instrument that God uses is not primary (1 Cor. 3:7).

Do miraculous gifts exist today? Both Scripture and experience answer a resounding no. Those who claim that such gifts are for today are wrong. In their zeal to promote God, they are teaching error. We must all remember that error leads away from God. The Spirit of God, the Spirit of power, is also the Spirit of truth. One cannot sacrifice the truth without grieving the Holy Spirit (Eph. 4:30; 6:17).

8

Was the Miracle From God or From Satan

?

The Bible and experience confirm that Satan works miracles. Because he is the king of deception (John 8:44; 2 Thess. 2:9, 10) and desires to mask his servants as "ministers of righteousness" (2 Cor. 11:13–15), it is vital that Christians have a way of discovering what is actually from God and what is from the devil. Jesus warned, "For there shall arise false Christs, and false prophets, and shall shew great signs and wonders; insomuch that, if it were possible, they shall deceive the very elect" (Matt. 24:24). We cannot afford to be ignorant of or reluctant to apply the biblical tests to all alleged miracles.

This is easier said than done. Many today need some crutch with which to support their faith. Such people seek for some physical or tangible evidence to substantiate their beliefs. Thus, if they ever have an experience involving a display of superhuman power, they cling to it as a most treasured possession. To subject such an experience to testing seems to them to be like a step in unbelief. The following statement, made by a missionary relating miraculous events in the southern Philippines, is typical: "To dissect such an obvious working of God seems almost sacrilege. In the final analysis, one can only bow humbly before the sovereign Lord and give praise to him" (Otis 1980, 219).

We must never forget that it is God's declared will to subject alleged miracles to rigorous testing. When a New Testament person claimed to have a prophecy from God, he was not given free reign. Paul commanded that when one prophet spoke, the other prophets were to judge, that is, discern whether the one claiming to be a prophet was really inspired (1 Cor. 14:29–32). Some think that such testing would quench the Spirit. But this assumption could not be farther from the truth, for Paul declares that the only way to keep from quenching the Holy Spirit is to prove all prophecies and miracles, adhering only to those that pass the test (1 Thess. 5:19–21).

The testing of alleged miracles must be extensive and careful. Two questions must be answered. The first is, Has a miracle actually occurred? The second naturally follows: Was the miracle generated by good or evil supernatural forces?

When people analyze alleged miracles, what should be their frame of mind? This important question must also be answered. Many see miracles because they want to see them, whereas others see no miracle because they refuse to believe that they can occur. The counsel of B. B. Warfield is most relevant: "The testimony to (a miracle's) occurrence should be carefully scrutinized and subjected to a thorough criticism. Until this is done, we naturally and properly receive the alleged fact with a certain suspension of judgment" (Warfield 1976, 190).

Neither unbridled optimism nor doubting pessimism should obscure our objective analysis of an alleged miracle. Rather, we should suspend all judgment until our research has been completed. This is proper, because when dealing with an alleged miracle we are dealing with a claim that involves God. We are not interested in examining the miracles of the occult.

They are overtly declared to be the productions of the devil. It is those miracles that claim God's authorship that must be carefully scrutinized. The reason for this is obvious. We dare not give the glory of God to another. If we claim that God wrought an act that in fact was performed by deception or demonic power, then we have committed a great sin. Through our haste to exalt him we have unknowingly substituted the creature into that glorious and exalted majesty of the Creator. Likewise, if we deny that the Lord has wrought a wonder when he evidently has, then we also are guilty of great sin. It behooves us all, then, to take great care in testing all claims of miracle working.

Second-Hand Accounts

The less obvious the miracle is, the more careful has to be its analysis. When we hear or read about an alleged miracle, we enter the world of testimony. The more times a story is repeated, the more likely it is that facts have been altered. It is amazing how readily stories of miraculous happenings are accepted and repeated. Very little verification occurs, because such questions are often interpreted as questioning the veracity or thoroughness of the witness or as personal attacks. Therefore, we should be sensitive and let it be known that duty to God and truth demands that we carefully investigate all such miraculous claims. Our questions do not arise from any motive other than our love of God.

If we repeat an unverified account, we are in fact bearing false witness. Whether or not we think it is an important issue, declaring something false to be true is a serious thing. It is an offense against the Word and nature of God. Zechariah states, "Speak ye every man the truth to his neighbor" (Zech. 8:16). Our God is a God of truth (John 14:6). He commands us to seek for truth, obtain it, and never to relinquish it (Prov. 23:23). For his sake, then, we must verify accounts of alleged miracles before we repeat them.

Verifying the Testimony

When analyzing the testimony of others, certain rules are to be followed. Summarizing the writing of Charles Hodge (C. Hodge 1960, 1:634), I suggest the following:

1. The witnesses must be able to prove their claims by sufficient evidence. If someone claims to have seen a man raised from the dead, we must seek more information. Was the man actually dead or simply unconscious? When, where, and under what conditions did it take place? We hear much about resurrections in China and Indonesia. These accounts should not be repeated as factual without such evidence in hand. The testimony of a person who has no such evidence is of no value. All the apostles gave witness of the resurrection of Christ based upon such solid evidence, stating names and places (Acts 1:3; 2:31, 32; 1 Cor. 15:3–8; John 20:19–29; 1 John 1:1–5).

2. The witnesses themselves should be rational and intelligent. They should be mentally capable of discerning the truthfulness of the event of which they testify. If the witnesses are of such an age or nature as to cause doubt of their ability to judge the event, their testimony is tarnished.

3. The witnesses themselves should be of good moral character. If their lives be suspect of immorality or deceit, their testimony is also suspect. If the alleged miracle leads to the financial benefit of the witness, the account is questionable. The love of money leads to all types of evil involving alleged miracles (Acts 8:18–23; 1 Tim. 6:10).

4. The event must be a possible event. Certain things are impossible. No amount of testimony can prove that two plus two ever equaled five. God cannot lie (Titus 1:2); he can never directly lead men to sin (James 1:13, 14); he cannot oppose himself or that which he has revealed of himself in his nature or Word (2 Tim. 2:13; Ps. 138:2). As such things are declared to be impossible, no testimony in support of them could ever be true. When Jim Jones declared that God had revealed to him that all his followers should commit suicide and force their

children to drink poison, he was in error. Who knows? He might have had a vision or been told to do this by a super-human being. But we are certain that it was not of God. It is an impossibility that the author of life, the God who said, "Thou shalt not kill," would lead a man to advocate mass murder. Unfortunately, the hundreds involved in Guyana would never question the declarations of their leader.

5. The event must be capable of being proven beyond any reasonable doubt. A miracle is an event in the physical world. All divine miracles are wrought for the advancement of God's glory. How is God's glory enhanced by anything involving obscurity or uncertainty? There is no conceivable reason why any such event should lack sufficient evidence. Christ's walking on water, or instantly healing the diseased, crippled, and blind were easily verifiable. The miracles of his apostles—unschooled Galileans speaking foreign languages fluently, casting out demons without a struggle in the name of Christ, healing all types of sicknesses in his name—could all be easily proven.

If these five rules were followed, a host of stories would be stopped for being either unverifiable or unworthy of repetition. God's glory is the issue to us as Christians. We refuse to allow anything beneath his divine dignity to be ascribed to him. Therefore, we should charitably but firmly apply these rules whenever we hear of an alleged miracle. The witness and the story must be carefully analyzed.

Verifying the Miracle

When verifying the evidence of an alleged miracle, it is imperative that we keep in mind the examples of miracles in God's Word. They were real miracles. Comparison, then, ought to be made between the alleged and the real.

1. We recommend that one seeks no higher cause for an event than what is necessary to produce it. If any event can be explained as occurring by any natural cause, then no miraculous cause should be claimed. If science offers a plausible

explanation for the occurrence of any event, we will accept it. (See appendix 3 for an interesting application of this rule to today's alleged speaking in tongues.) The God of miracles is the God of nature. He is the author of truth wherever it may be found. The verifiable facts of science will never contradict the facts of Christianity. Science is not the enemy of Christianity. On the other hand, it should never be utilized through unbelief simply to explain away a miraculous event, as many modern skeptics have done. The attempts of theological liberals to strip the miracles from the Bible is a futile effort grounded in ignorance and pride. It deeply offends both God and his children.

2. If an event is not obviously a miracle, then we should not struggle to prove that it is a miracle. A miracle is clearly a wonder.

3. If an event has any questionable marks of secrecy about it, then it should not be claimed as miraculous. Archibald Alexander wrote:

> The miracles of Jesus were performed, for the most part in an open and public manner, in the presence of multitudes of witnesses, under the inspection of learned and malignant enemies, in a variety of circumstances, and for several years in succession. There was here no room for trick, sleight of hand, illusion of the senses, or anything else which could impose on the spectators (A. Alexander 1836, 99–100).

Any reluctance to allow critics to test the veracity of a miracle is a strong evidence of foul play. When a miracle has been performed, there should be no fear to test it. The results of the test will bear witness to the authenticity of the miracle, thereby establishing its reality with greater force. The testimony of believers carries a limited power. But the testimony of unbelieving critics is absolutely shattering, as when the Jewish leaders said, "What shall we do to these men? for that indeed a notable miracle hath been done by them is manifest to all them that dwell in Jerusalem; and we cannot deny it" (Acts 4:16).

Verifying the Source

Once we are certain that a legitimate miracle has occurred, our work has just begun. We must then apply the following tests, which help us decide whether or not the miracle was of God. One key point in discerning the source of a miracle is to consider the person involved in its occurrence. A miraculous event is not to be separated from its context. If the activities surrounding a miracle are erroneous or immoral, the source of the miracle is not the God of truth and holiness. Miracles rarely occur apart from some teacher. The teacher is teaching truth or error. Miracles accompanying the teaching, prayers, or other activities of this person reveal the connection between him or her and the source of the miracle. The miracle and its entire context form a unit that reveals the true power behind the miracle. This is one rule in discerning the cause behind miracles.

The Word of God

The first test in discovering whether a miracle is of God involves God's Word. God will not work a miracle in support of a teaching that opposes his holy Word. Warfield affirmed that "the connection of alleged miracles with erroneous doctrine invalidates their claim to be genuine works of God" (Warfield 1972, 53). This is precisely what Moses, Paul, and John taught. Let us consider three main Bible passages.

> If there arise among you a prophet, or a dreamer of dreams, and giveth thee a sign or a wonder, and the sign or the wonder come to pass, whereof he spake unto thee, saying, Let us go after other gods, which thou hast not known, and let us serve them; thou shalt not hearken unto the words of that prophet, or that dreamer of dreams: for the LORD your God proveth you, to know whether ye love the LORD your God with all your heart and with all your soul. Ye shall walk after the LORD your God, and fear him, and keep his commandments, and obey his voice, and ye shall serve him, and cleave unto him. And that

prophet, or that dreamer of dreams, shall be put to death; because he hath spoken to turn you away from the LORD your God, which brought you out of the land of Egypt, and redeemed you out of the house of bondage, to thrust thee out of the way which the LORD thy God commanded thee to walk in. So shalt thou put the evil away from the midst of thee (Deut. 13:1–5).

In this very important passage we see a warning against a miracle worker. The people were not to believe or obey him if he taught them anything contrary to what God had taught them. The false prophet's appearance among them was a test of their love of God. Would the people of God follow the false prophet, mesmerized by his acts of power, or would they continue in the commandments of the Lord? If the people were ignorant of God's Word, they would have no safety against such evil workers. They would not have a standard by which to test his teaching. Also, if they forgot that a miracle could be caused by an evil source, their souls would be in grave danger. The same rule applies today.

But though we, or an angel from heaven, preach any other gospel unto you than that which we have preached unto you, let him be accursed. As we said before, so say I now again, If any man preach any other gospel unto you than that ye have received, let him be accursed (Gal. 1:8, 9).

Charles Hodge commented:

No amount of learning, no superiority of talent, nor even the pretension to inspiration, can justify a departure from the . . . truths taught by men to whose inspiration God has borne witness. All teachers must be brought to this standard; and even if an angel from heaven should teach anything contrary to the Scriptures, he should be regarded as anathema, Gal. 1:8. It is a matter of constant gratitude that we have such a standard whereby to try the spirits whether they be of God (C. Hodge 1972, 395).

Another interesting point about this passage is that Paul includes himself among those who deserve to be condemned if he changes his doctrine and proclaims a different gospel. This affirms that God's people must stand vigilant at all times. They must constantly test the doctrines preached to them by the great standard, the Bible. Age and experience do not guarantee one will not preach error. Every teaching must be brought "to the law and to the testimony: if they speak not according to this word, it is because there is no light in them" (Isa. 8:20).

Again, Charles Hodge wrote:

> John commands Christians, "Believe not every spirit, but try the spirits whether they are of God: because many false prophets are gone out into the world," 1 John 4:1. And the standard by which these prophets were to be tried, he gives in verse 6: "We are of God: he that knoweth God heareth us; he that is not of God heareth not us. Hereby we know the spirit of truth, and the spirit of error." It was obviously necessary that Christians, in the age of immediate inspiration, should have some means of discriminating between those who were really under the influence of the Spirit of God, and those who were either enthusiasts or deceivers. And the test to which the apostles directed them was rational, and easily applied. These were the inspired men to whose divine mission and authority God had borne abundant testimony by "signs and wonders, and divers miracles, and gifts of the Holy Spirit." As God cannot contradict himself, it follows that anything inconsistent with the teachings of these men, though proceeding from one claiming to be a prophet, must be false, and the pretension of its author to inspiration unfounded (C. Hodge 1972, 391).

The apostle Paul said, "If any man think himself to be a prophet, or spiritual, let him acknowledge that the things that I write unto you are the commandments of the Lord" (1 Cor. 14:37). To deviate from the teaching of an apostle was to forsake the teaching of Christ (see Acts 1:1, 2; 1 Thess. 2:13).

The first and major test, then, of the source of any miracle is to analyze the doctrine of the miracle worker. If the doctrine attested to by the miracle opposes any fundamental truth of Scripture, the person working the wonder is either deceived or a deceiver. The source of such miracle-working power is demonic. God will not oppose himself. Those performing his works will teach his doctrine.

B. B. Warfield wrestled with the alleged miraculous cures recorded at Lourdes, France. These miracles were surrounded by Mariolatry (the worship of Mary); therefore, they could not be of God. The following statement has special application today, as the Roman Catholic Church, still advocating false doctrine, alleges numerous miracles from shrines all over the world:

> Even though we should stand dumb before the wonders of Lourdes, and should be utterly incapable of suggesting a natural causation for them, we know right well they are not of God. The whole complex of circumstances of which they are a part . . . stamp them, prior to all examination of the mode of their occurrence, as not from God (Warfield 1972, 122).

It is important also to mention the incarnate Word, Jesus Christ (John 1:1, 14). He is the will of God personified. He who was eternally "in the bosom of the Father, he hath declared him" (John 1:18). A person who denies the deity or lordship of Jesus Christ denies God (see 1 Cor. 12:3; 1 John 2:22, 23; 4:2, 3). The incarnate Word and the written Word never contradict each other. They are both the revelation of God. Wherever Christ or his Word are opposed, denied or compromised, there is the work of evil. No divine miracle can grow out of that soil.

The Nature of God

The second test to be applied to miracles regards the nature of God. Scripture teaches that the nature of God is seen in the world, which he created (Psalm 19:1; Rom. 1:20). Is it wrong for us to expect the same of his miraculous works? Certainly not. What are we to think of an event that is declared to be an act of God but manifests symptoms that oppose the nature of God? A tree is known by its fruit, and God is known by all his marvelous works. He is glorified by what he does. Anyone who refuses to exalt or glorify God alone is not a true servant of the Lord. And any act that opposes the nature of God as revealed in his Word cannot be an act of God. Let me illustrate through two aspects of his nature.

First is God's power. God is omnipotent. Nebuchadnezzar declared, "And all the inhabitants of the earth are reputed as nothing: and he doeth according to his will in the army of heaven, and among the inhabitants of the earth: and none can stay his hand, or say unto him, What doest thou?" (Dan. 4:35). The great multitude in heaven say, "Alleluia: for the Lord God omnipotent reigneth" (Rev. 19:6). When Jesus worked miracles, the mighty power of God was evident. No contrary wind, crippling disease, or evil spirit could withstand his power. He never failed, because his miracles were the works of the almighty God.

But what are we to think of the alleged miracles being exalted today? Is omnipotence revealed when the sick are not fully recovered? Or when demons resist the command to come out of the demonized? Or worse, when they regularly return and repossess the ones delivered? There are very many claims of miracles today, but few are the evident manifestations of God's omnipotence.

Second is God's wisdom. God is omniscient. There is nothing unwise in him. For this reason he is declared to be a God of order and not the author of confusion (1 Cor. 14:33, 40). No miraculous event, characterized by either disorder or confusion, is his work.

Warfield well summarizes this whole point, stating:

> God is not bare omnipotence; He is absolute omniscience as well. He cannot possibly be the immediate agent in an act in which a gross failure of "wisdom" is apparent, no matter how difficult it may be for us to explain that act without calling in omnipotence as its producing cause. Still less can He be supposed to be the immediate actor in occurrences in which immoralities are implicated; or, in which . . . there are embodied implications of, say, irreligion or of superstition. Whether we

can see how such occurrences are wrought, or not, we know from the outset that God did not work them (Warfield 1972, 121).

The Fruit of God's Spirit

The third major test to be applied to a miracle involves the fruit of the Spirit of God. What happens when a person declares to be under the special, direct influence of God and at the same time lives in immorality? We must conclude that such a person is at best self-deceived and at worst demonized. The Spirit of God is the Spirit of holiness. He can be grieved (Eph. 4:30) and quenched (1 Thess. 5:19) by sin. Inward and outward purity are graciously wrought in the life of him who is "a vessel unto honor, sanctified, and meet [fit] for the master's use, and prepared unto every good work" (2 Tim. 2:21).

Jesus said, "Beware of false prophets, which come to you in sheep's clothing, but inwardly they are ravening wolves. Ye shall know them by their fruits" (Matt. 7:15, 16). If they do not manifest the fruit of the Holy Spirit, they are not ministering under the power of the Holy Spirit. The following texts help give us direction in discerning whether or not a miracle worker is of God:

> Now the works of the flesh are manifest, which are these: Adultery, fornication, uncleanness, lasciviousness, idolatry, witchcraft, hatred, variance, emulations, wrath, strife, seditions, heresies, envyings, murders, drunkenness, revellings, and such like: of the which I tell you before, as I have told you in time past, that they which do such things shall not inherit the kingdom of God. But the fruit of the Spirit is love, joy, peace, longsuffering, gentleness, goodness, faith, meekness, temperance: against such there is no law. And they that are Christ's have crucified the flesh with the affections and lusts (Gal. 5:19–24).

> For ye were sometimes darkness, but now are ye light in the Lord: walk as children of light: (for the fruit of the Spirit is in all goodness and righteousness and truth;) proving what is acceptable unto the Lord. And have no fellowship with the unfruitful works of darkness, but rather reprove them (Eph. 5:8–11).

This is a true saying. If a man desire the office of a bishop, he desireth a good work. A bishop then must be blameless, the husband of one wife, vigilant, sober, of good behavior, given to hospitality, apt to teach; not given to wine, no striker, not greedy of filthy lucre; but patient, not a brawler, not covetous; one that ruleth well his own house, having his children in subjection with all gravity; (for if a man know not how to rule his own house, how shall he take care of the church of God?) Not a novice, lest being lifted up with pride he fall into the condemnation of the devil. Moreover he must have a good report of them which are without; lest he fall into reproach and the snare of the devil (1 Tim. 3:1–7).

Who is a wise man and endued with knowledge among you? let him shew out of a good conversation his works with meekness of wisdom. But if ye have bitter envying and strife in your hearts, glory not, and lie not against the truth. This wisdom descendeth not from above, but is earthly, sensual, devilish. For where envying and strife is, there is confusion and every evil work. But the wisdom that is from above is first pure, then peaceable, gentle, and easy to be entreated, full of mercy and good fruits, without partiality, and without hypocrisy. And the fruit of righteousness is sown in peace of them that make peace (James 3:13–18).

Sinless perfection is not required of Christians, but freedom from the bondage of all sin is required. An unbeliever holds and cherishes sin. The believer is still a sinner, but one over whom "sin shall not have dominion" (Rom. 6:14). He will occasionally slip and fall (Ps. 37:23, 24); but will not remain in the path of sin. Those who habitually walk in any sin are the servants of sin (Rom. 6:16–18). If a person performs a self-exalting miracle while living in immorality, that miracle was not wrought by the Holy Spirit of God.

The Scriptures teach that many miracle workers, professing themselves to be Christians, will be shocked to discover that the miracles they performed in Christ's name were fraudulent and that they themselves are not born again Christians. Jesus said:

Not every one that saith unto me, Lord, Lord, shall enter into the kingdom of heaven; but he that doeth the will of my Father which is in heaven. Many will say to me in that day, Lord, Lord, have we not prophesied in thy name? and in thy name have cast out demons? and in thy name have done many wonderful works? And then will I profess unto them, I never knew you: depart from me, ye that work iniquity (Matt. 7:21–23).

The problem with the above-mentioned people could only be discerned by looking at the final product of their labors. They were aiding, perhaps unknowingly, the kingdom of darkness. In many ways these resemble true laborers of Christ, but the end product is ungodly. Charles Hodge well said:

The recompense of every man, shall not be according to his professions, not according to his own convictions or judgment of his character or conduct, not according to appearances or the estimates of men, but according to his works. If men really promote the kingdom of Christ, they will be regarded and treated as his servants; if they increase the dominion of sin and error, they will be regarded as ministers of Satan (C. Hodge n.d., 265).

Paul speaks of those who "profess that they know God; but in works deny him" (Titus 1:16). A work of God is not characterized simply by power, but also and primarily by holiness and truth (see appendix 4 for comments on the strange union of the charismatic movement with the Roman Catholic Church and the World Council of Churches).

Summary

When investigating a miracle we should first establish that a real miracle has occurred. If the report has come by another's testimony, we must not only analyze the evidence, but also the person testifying to the miracle.

When a miracle has unquestionably occurred, our great duty

is to ascertain if the generating power was God or Satan. As we have shown, this can be done by carefully analyzing the miracle and the miracle worker in the light of the Word of God, the nature of God, and the fruit of the Spirit of God. The process of investigation may demand great patience, but God will richly reward all those who thus sincerely seek for truth out of devotion to him. Through the prophet Jeremiah, God said, "Run ye to and fro through the streets of Jerusalem, and see now, and know, and seek in the broad places thereof, if ye can find a man, if there be any that . . . seeketh the truth; and I will pardon it" (Jer. 5:1). Love of the truth will be the great test of character and faith in that awful day when Satan's miracle-working agent reigns in the world, as Paul prophesied: "And then shall that Wicked be revealed . . . even him, whose coming is after the working of Satan with all power and signs and lying wonders . . . in them that perish; *because they received not the love of the truth,* that they might be saved" (2 Thess. 2:8–10, italics added).

Take heed, my friends, and be not deceived.

9

Was That Experience From God

?

The Christian life is a full and wonderful life. The promises of God cover "the life that now is, and of that which is to come" (1 Tim. 4:8). Therefore, we should not wait until we go to heaven to start enjoying salvation. Christ provides the Christian with a lifetime of glorious experiences. The emotions of joy, peace, love, and compassion that accompany the filling of the Spirit of God are indescribable. Through the gracious influences of the Spirit the Christian enjoys an unparalleled growth in every dimension of life. The spiritual dimension bursts forth with new feelings and experiences.

What standard is there by which the Christian discerns what experiences are good and what are evil? Or has the Lord ordained us to learn only by our own mistakes? No. He loves us far too much to abandon us to a trial-and-error method of Christian growth.

The church of past ages knew where to go for guidance concerning religious experiences. They went to the Word of God.

The Bible is not simply a divine book of doctrine. It is also a perfect and complete commentary on Christian life. The West-minster Confession of Faith affirms the Bible to be "the rule of faith and life." Declaring this truth, Archibald Alexander wrote:

> In judging of religious experience it is all important to keep steadily in view the system of divine truth contained in the Holy Scriptures; otherwise, our experience, as is too often the case, will degenerate into enthusiasm. Many ardent professors seem too readily to take it for granted that all religious feeling must be good. They therefore take no care to discriminate between the genuine and the spurious, the pure gold and tinsel. Their only concern is about the ardour of their feeings; not considering that if they are spurious, the more intense they are, the further will they lead them astray (A. Alexander 1967, xviii).

The tendency in our day of spiritual impoverishment is to elevate each religious experience as an unquestionable blessing of God. Then the experience is superimposed upon the Bible as a proof of its legitimacy. If it does not fit exactly, we force it into place like Cinderella's stepsisters trying to put on the glass slipper. This practice is

> what Martyn Lloyd-Jones calls "capitulation to phenomena." This is the error of allowing one's doctrine to be determined by phenomena. The facts cannot be gainsaid, so it is decided that they must be accomodated by theology and therefore theology is adjusted accordingly. But it is not necessary to do this. On the contrary, the Christian should seek to interpret facts in the light of the teaching of Scripture. He must not allow phenomena to determine his belief (Leahy 1975, 166).

The Bible itself claims to give inspired guidance in how we are to live, not merely in what we are to believe. Therefore, Jesus, quoting Deut. 8:3, said, "Man shall not live by bread alone, but by every word that proceedeth out of the mouth of God" (Matt. 4:4). This could not be more clearly stated than it is by Paul in 2 Timothy 3:16, 17: "All scripture is given by inspira-tion of God, and is profitable for doctrine, for reproof, for correc-tion, for instruction in righteousness; that the man of God may be perfect, thoroughly furnished unto all good works."

Scripture is here declared to be profitable for doctrine and life, establishing a perfect guide for both truth and good works. The standard by which we discern true teaching is the same as that by which we understand legitimate religious experiences. The Christian is bound to receive as authentic only that which parallels the approved experiences of believers as recorded in the Bible.

Alexander again stated:

> In our day there is nothing more necessary than to distinguish carefully between true and false experiences of religion; to "try the spirits whether they are of God." And in making this discrimination, that there is no other test but the infallible Word of God; let every thought, motive, impulse and emotion be brought to this touchstone. "To the law and the testimony; if they speak not according to these, it is because there is no light in them" (A. Alexander 1967, xviii).

If this was true over one hundred years ago, it is more so today. Then there were few who were claiming miraculous experiences. Today there are millions who believe themselves to be supernaturally led and empowered by the Holy Spirit. The need to authenticate this claim in a biblical manner is evident. For if they are the Spirit's vessels, we had better hear and follow their words. But if they are deluded, be it ever so innocently, it is vital that they realize this deception and turn away from it.

Slain in the Spirit

Let's apply this rule to a rather familiar experience in some Christian groups: being slain in the Spirit. This often follows the laying on of hands or some intense religious activity. This experience was described by Aimee Semple McPherson as follows (quoted by Bruner):

> "Three received the baptism that night. One lady fell by the organ, another at the side of the church. . . . The third night nineteen received the baptism of the Holy Spirit. Down they

went right and left, between the seats, in the aisles, in front of the chancel rail, up on the platform. . . . It was only a few minutes later while praying—with the seekers, and they were going down one by one under the mighty rushing wind of the heavenly gales that were sweeping from heaven, that we heard a great shout, and something struck the floor with a thump. . . . [It was] the trustee who had but shortly before declared that all of this noise and shouting was unnecessary. I doubt if there was anyone in the church who made as much noise as he. He shook from head to foot; his face was aglow with heaven's light; he fairly shouted and roared forth as the Spirit gave him utterance, as his heart was filled with joy and glory" (Bruner 1970, 125, 126).

The symptoms of this experience usually include a falling to the ground, temporary unconsciousness, and convulsing. This experience is not unique to twentieth-century Pentecostalism. Charles Hodge described the same experience as follows:

They began with what was called the falling exercise; that is, the person affected would fall on the ground helpless as an infant. This was soon succeeded, in many places, by a species of convulsions called the jerks. Sometimes it would affect the whole body, jerking it violently from place to place, regardless of all obstacles; at others a single limb would be agitated. . . . These exercises were evidently involuntary. They were highly infectious, and spread rapidly from place to place; often seizing on mere spectators, and even upon those who abhorred and dreaded them (C. Hodge 1851, 77).

It is evident that similar experiences happen in totally unreligious contexts. During the 1960s, for instance, it was not uncommon for a teenaged girl to have a like experience when attending a concert featuring Elvis Presley or the Beatles. Fainting spells and convulsions are common phenomena in all parts of the world wherever there is religious fanaticism, whether it be pagan, cultic, or within the professing Christian church.

What shall we say about such an experience? The Princeton

theologians, after examining the experience in light of the Scriptures, came to an unshakable conclusion that it was not the work of the Holy Spirit. Many today would object to this conclusion. But Charles Hodge reveals the solid biblical basis for this conclusion by writing:

> This view of the subject is greatly confirmed by the consideration, that there is nothing in the Bible to lead us to regard these bodily affections as the legitimate effects of religious feeling. No such results followed the preaching of Christ or his apostles. We hear of no general outcries, faintings, convulsions, or ravings in the assemblies which they addressed. . . .
>
> The testimony of the Scriptures is not merely negative on this subject. Their authority is directly opposed to all such disorders. They direct that all things should be done decently and in order. They teach us that God is not the author of confusion, but of peace, in all the churches of the saints (1 Cor. 14:33, 40). These passages have particular reference to the manner of conducting public worship. They forbid everything which is inconsistent with order, solemnity, and devout attention. It is evident that loud outcries and convulsions are inconsistent with these things, and therefore ought to be discouraged. They cannot come from God, for He is not the author of confusion (C. Hodge 1851, 80).

Many noncharismatics ascribe this experience to demons. Whether or not such an experience is demonic cannot easily be determined. In some cases its source is overcharged emotion. In other cases it may be demonic interference. Remember, the safe rule is that demonic agency should never hastily be ascribed if the phenomenon in question can be explained by human agency. Since an abnormal state of the human spirit can account for all the symptoms of being "slain in the Spirit," we must not overreact and dogmatically call it demonic.

Should We Take Chances with the Spirit?

John Wimber explains why many Western Christians have not experienced miracles, saying, "Resisting what they cannot fully control or always understand, they miss out on doing Christ's works today" (Wimber 1986, 81). This, I believe, truly identifies two basic obstacles many of us have with these experiences. The first obstacle involves self-control; the other obstacle relates to knowledge.

When people abandon themselves over to an unproven spiritual power, for whatever reason, like to be "baptized with the Holy Spirit" or in search of greater personal power, they are taking a chance. There is a type of spiritual gamble that occurs, because the outcome is not certain. Wimber realizes this and states, "As Christians learn and see that there is more to experience, they are willing to take a chance, step out in faith, and receive God's power" (Wimber 1986, 147). In his booklet "Seven Vital Steps to Receiving the Holy Spirit" Kenneth Hagin begins step five by saying:

> Tell the candidate to throw away all of his fears that he has acquired from foolish teachers that have made him afraid. Tell him not to fear receiving something which is false or counterfeit. There is no danger of receiving anything false. God does not lie and He has said that if we ask, He will give the Holy Spirit to us (Hagin 1978, 5).

The problem is that since the miraculous gifts are no longer given, then the possibility of counterfeit and demonic deception in these experiences is greatly increased. Thus, there is every reason for those who seek such an experience to do so with fear and uncertainty.

There seems to be a major oversight in this whole argument: self-control is the gift of the Holy Spirit (Gal. 5:23). This gift is not to be thrown away for any reason. Would God offer a spiritual gift to us which demands that we sacrifice one of the characteristics of the Spirit of God which he has wrought within us? Of course not.

When Paul wrote to Corinth, he stressed the need for self-control when one exercised the spiritual gifts. When the true gifts of the Spirit were possessed, the individual never lost self-control and rational aptitude. There was no chance involved when the true gift of prophecy was given, Paul taught, because "the spirits of the prophets are subject to the prophets" (1 Cor. 14:32). In other words, even the prophets of God were self-controlled in the midst of their prophesying. They were never seized with some irresistible force that overcame their individual personalities. To the same Corinthians he said:

> And every man that striveth in the games exerciseth self-control in all things. Now they do it to receive a corruptible crown; but we an incorruptible. I therefore so run, as not uncertainly; so fight I, as not beating the air: but I buffet my body, and bring it into bondage: lest by any means, after that I have preached to others, I myself should be rejected (1 Cor. 9:25–27 ASV).

So Paul viewed loss of self-control as a step toward disqualification in the service of the Lord. We certainly lay a dangerous foundation if when seeking the Spirit we oppose the way of the Spirit. This is true of any who seek a spiritual experience at the price of temperance (self-control).

Understanding is also an obstacle to these miraculous gifts, according to many. Wimber again states, "Tongues, prophecy, words of knowledge—many of the experiences I have described in this book—are an assault on Western Christians' predilection toward personal control of their experience. We find security in the predictable, intellectually understandable experience" (Wimber 1986, 150, 151).

We must remember, however, that part of man's being made in the image of God is the gift of intellectual aptitude. We are thinking, rational creatures. This ability is increased, not decreased, as a result of our spiritual regeneration (Eph. 4:23, 24; Col. 3:10). Indeed, one of the distinguishing marks of a mature Christian is the ability to think with careful discernment, as the author of Hebrews writes: "For every one that useth milk is unskilful in the word of righteousness: for he is a babe. But strong meat belongeth to them that are of full age, even those who by reason of use have their senses exercised to discern both good and evil" (Heb. 5:13, 14; see 2 Tim. 1:7).

The very two characteristics that are supposed by many charismatics to be hindrances to spiritual development and advanced Christian experiences—self-control and understanding—are declared by Peter and Paul to be proof of spiritual maturity. Peter counsels, "And besides this, giving all diligence, add to your faith virtue; and to virtue knowledge; and to knowledge temperance" (2 Peter 1:5, 6). These are characteristics that are to be added to, not subtracted from our Christian lives. Paul told Titus: "But speak thou the things which become sound doctrine: that the aged men be sober, grave, temperate. . . . Young men likewise exhort to be sober minded" (Titus 2:1, 2, 6).

Sound doctrine is not advanced when self-control and knowledge are diminished. To serve God is a reasonable or rational thing to do (Rom. 12:1). Faith, therefore, does not run counter to reason. Faith involves affirming in the mind that something is true. Belief in something or someone demands evidence (Heb. 11:1). It is the office of reason to examine such evidence and determine its trustworthiness. Faith and fact go hand-in-hand. We must never remove our faith from the foundation of objective evidence. Charles Hodge beautifully explains: "Christians, therefore, concede to reason all the prerogatives it can rightfully claim. God requires nothing irrational of his rational creatures. He does not require faith without knowledge, nor faith without evidence" (C. Hodge 1960, 1:50).

The only safe refuge for the Christian to resort to, when analyzing the legitimacy of an experience, is the Word of God. The comparison made between the alleged and the truly biblical experience must be honest and thorough. It is not enough for people to claim to have biblical experiences. We must test those claims by a careful analysis.

It is also not a sufficient guard that a person be a thoroughly sincere individual. Sincerity does not necessarily preclude one from error. Saul of Tarsus was sincerely performing what he thought was God's will when he persecuted the church. He later lamented that the Jews "have a zeal of God, but not according to knowledge" (Rom. 10:2). Sincerity or zeal without truth leads to bondage. One is made free only by knowledge of truth, as Jesus said: "And ye shall know the truth, and the truth shall make you free" (John 8:32). Hodge well said:

> Many men honestly believe themselves to be inspired, who are under the influence of some evil spirit,—their own it may be. . . . Irresistible conviction is not enough. It may satisfy the subject of it himself. But it cannot satisfy others, or be a criterion of truth. Thousands have been, and still are, fully convinced that the false is true, and that what is wrong is right (C. Hodge 1960, 1:102).

So, uncertainty need not plague us when analyzing our own or others' spiritual experiences. Only those are legitimately from God that bear his stamp of approval. If they follow the experiences enjoyed by normal believers as revealed in the Bible, then they are of God. And the roots of all truly Christian experiences have ever been prayer and Bible study. Through these channels God gives whatever grace we need day by day. If we go beyond this, we are forced to take unwarranted and dangerous chances that might result in great harm.

For instance, Nadab and Abihu took a chance (Lev. 10:1–5). They wanted to worship God. Fine. But they decided on coming to God in a different and new way. It wasn't altogether different, just a little different, a little daring, a little experiment. They offered incense to God but lit the incense from a common fire rather than from the fire off the altar. Nadab and Abihu were immediately slain by God for performing this novel act of worship. God does not want us to experiment with our souls or his worship. He wants us to obey his Word in our worship and experiences.

10

Why Does God
Allow Satanic Miracles
?

We are greatly comforted from realizing, through Job 1 and 2, that Satan cannot attack believers unless permitted to do so by the Lord. The devil is not sovereign on this earth. He is on a leash, which we call the permissive will of God. Paul assures us that everything, even Satan's malevolent activity, will somehow work for our good and God's glory (Rom. 8:28).

Satan and his demons did not cease being creatures when they fell. Their efforts and designs are all subject to the sovereign will of their Creator, as are the lives of all creatures (Prov. 16:9, 33). Paul exalts Christ, declaring, "For by him were all things created, that are in heaven, and that are in earth, visible and invisible, whether they be thrones, or dominions, or principalities, or powers: all things were created by him, and for him" (Col. 1:16).

Whatever miracles Satan performs are permitted by God and form a part of his omniscient, inscrutable plan. The sinfulness behind them belongs solely to the devil. Satan's desire to deceive and ensnare, therefore, is realized only within the boundaries prescribed by God (2 Thess. 2:10–12). We know the elect can never be fully and finally led astray by them (Matt. 24:24). What is certainly true of man's sinful acts is true of Satan's sinful acts: "Surely the wrath of man shall praise thee: the remainder of wrath shalt thou restrain" (Psalm 76:10). God permits only such sin as will, in some amazing form or way, eventually lead to exalting and glorifying himself. Joseph's brothers meant it for evil when they sold their brother into slavery, "but God meant it unto good, to bring to pass, as it is this day, to save much people alive" (Gen. 50:20). All we can do is reverently bow to such a God as this and declare with the humbled king:

> He doeth according to his will in the army of heaven, and among the inhabitants of the earth: and none can stay his hand, or say unto him, What doest thou? . . . Now I Nebuchadnezzar praise and extol and honor the King of heaven, all whose works are truth, and his ways judgment: and those that walk in pride he is able to abase (Dan. 4:35, 37).

Avoid the Extremes

There are two extreme positions that we must guard against when dealing with satanic miracles. One tendency is to represent the relationship between God and Satan in such a way that God seems to become the author of sin. In their earnest attempt to preserve the doctrine of God's sovereignty, some have seemingly implicated him as the direct cause of the evil that exists. This dangerous imbalance can lead to the spirit adopted by the "sons of thunder," and reproved by Christ when he affirmed: "Ye know not what manner of spirit ye are of. For the Son of man is not come to destroy men's lives, but to save them" (Luke 9:55, 56). God does not say the following with "tongue in cheek": "Say unto them, As I live, saith the Lord GOD, I have no pleasure in the death of the wicked; but that the wicked turn from his way and live: turn ye, turn ye from your evil ways; for why will ye die, O house of Israel?" (Ezek. 33:11; also Matt. 23:37; 2 Peter 3:9; Rev. 22:17).

It would be good for every budding Calvinist to regard the

counsel of the Westminster Divines who stated: "The doctrine of this high mystery of predestination is to be carefully handled with special prudence and care. . . ." (Confession of Faith III:8). James declares that "God cannot be tempted with evil, neither tempteth he any man" (James 1:13). We must be as careful to guard God's holiness in our statements as we are zealous to promote his sovereignty.

The other extreme occurs when men represent the works of the devil as if they were totally outside of God's will and control. Some portray God as having a kind of hands-off policy concerning the devil. They refuse to believe that God has anything to do with Satan. Of course, if this were true, then God would be limited in his power and reign. These people are sincerely attempting to remove God from in any way appearing to be connected with evil. Unfortunately, they do this in ways that strip God of his sovereignty, his power, his deity. The following is a typical example of this class of authors:

> First of all, is sickness God's will? A good way to address that question is to raise another one. Is sickness a kingdom value? Obviously not. As we have seen, it is as contrary to the life-style of the kingdom as is poverty or war.
>
> If sickness is not God's will, but many people in fact are sick, what is the cause? The answer clearly is Satan. I agree with Robert Wise, who says, "Let's mark the conclusion in red letters. The disasters of the world do not have their origin in the will of God. The evil one is the author of adversity" (Wagner 1988, 109).

What such people do not seem to realize is that the Bible teaches both that God is sinless, and that sin and Satan are permitted as a part of his plan. They are equal truths. There are certain truths like these that are impossible for mortals to fully comprehend. We are called upon to accept them by faith, because they are revealed as true. The Scriptures teach: "See now that I, even I, am he, and there is no god with me: I kill, and I make alive; I wound, and I heal: neither is there any that can deliver out of my hand" (Deut. 32:39). Again: "The LORD killeth, and maketh alive: he bringeth down to the grave, and bringeth up. The LORD maketh poor, and maketh rich: he bringeth low, and lifteth up" (1 Sam. 2:6, 7).

How can sickness, Satan, and a holy God be part of a single, consistent plan? There is only one explanation. Jesus touches on it when explaining the reason for Lazarus's death. He said, "This sickness is not unto death, but for the glory of God, that the Son of God might be glorified thereby" (John 11:4). The ultimate revelation of God's glory was more important, more basic than the immediate alleviation of Lazarus's condition. The friend of Jesus was allowed to die because God would be greatly glorified by his resurrection.

God is central; man is peripheral. Hence, the works of God are all ordered so as to manifest some aspect of his divine glory. It is not until we begin to appreciate and understand the concept of *the glory of God* that we truly understand the plan of God in this world.

The Glory of God

When dealing with this subject with my students, I have often read the following passages from Charles Hodge's *Systematic Theology*. The mere reading of these truths has often led immediately into a time of tearful prayer and worship. I trust that as you read them, the Lord will touch your heart with the profound light and power of his Word and nature.

> The final cause of all God's purposes is his own glory. This is frequently declared to be the end of all things. "Thou art worthy," say the heavenly worshippers, "O Lord, to receive glory, and honour, and power: for thou hast created all things, and for thy pleasure they are and were created" (Rev. 4:11). All things are said to be not only of God and through him, but for him (Rom. 11:36). He is the beginning and the end. The heavens declare his glory; that is the purpose for which they were made. God frequently announces his determination to make his glory

known. "As truly as I live, all the earth shall be filled with the glory of the LORD." (Num. 14:21.) This is also said to be the end of all the dispensations of his providence, whether beneficent or punitive. "For mine own sake, even for mine own sake, will I do it; for how should my name be polluted? and I will not give my glory unto another" (Isa. 48:11) . . . . In like manner the whole plan of redemption and the dispensations of his grace are declared to be designed to reveal the glory of God (1 Cor. 1:26–31; Eph. 3:8–10). This is the end which our Lord proposed to himself. He did everything for the glory of God; and for this end all his followers are required to live and act (Matt. 5:16; 1 Cor. 10:31).

As God is infinite and all his creatures are as nothing in comparison with him, it is plain that the revelation of his nature and perfections must be the highest conceivable end of all things, and the most conducive to secure all other good subordinate ends. Order and truth, however, depend on things being put in their right relations. If we make the good of the creature the ultimate object of all God's works, then we subordinate God to the creature, and endless confusion and unavoidable error are the consequence. It is characteristic of the Bible that it places God first, and the good of the creation second. This also is the characteristic feature of Augustinianism as distinguished from all other forms of doctrine (C. Hodge 1960, I:535, 536).

So whether we are talking about the topics of sickness, satanic miracles, the sunrise, or salvation, God's purpose is the same throughout. All that he does or permits to be done is for the further manifestation of his glorious nature. That was God's chief purpose in creating this world, and that has continued to be his plan in governing it. As Hodge again explains:

The Bible, Augustine, and the Reformed, give one answer to all such questions as the following: Why did God create the world? Why did he permit the occurrence of sin? Why was salvation provided for men and not for angels? Why was the knowledge of that salvation so long confined to one people? Why among those who hear the gospel, do some receive, and others reject it? To all these, and similar questions, the answer is, . . . Thus it seemed good in the eyes of God (Matt. 11:25, 26). Whatever he does or permits to be done, is done or permitted for the more perfect revelation of his nature and perfections. As the knowledge of God is the ground and sum of all good, it of course follows that the more perfectly God is known, the more fully the highest good . . . of the intelligent universe is promoted (C. Hodge 1960, III:536, 537).

You might ask, In what conceivable way is God glorified by permitting sin and deception in the world? The confusion is dispelled from our minds the moment we remember that God's nature is multifaceted. He is not merely a God of power, but also a God of love. He is not only a God of love, but also a God of holiness and justice. All his works, in some way, magnify some aspect of his glorious nature. Again Hodge teaches:

The knowledge of God is eternal life (John 17:3). It is for creatures the highest good. And the promotion of that knowledge, the manifestation of the manifold perfections of the infinite God, is the highest end of all his works. This is declared by the Apostle to be the end contemplated, both in the punishment of sinners and in the salvation of believers. It is an end to which, he says, no man can rationally object . . . (Rom. 9:22, 23). Sin, therefore, according to the Scriptures, is permitted that the justice of God may be known in its punishment, and his grace in its forgiveness. And the universe, without the knowledge of these attributes, would be like the earth without the light of the sun (C. Hodge 1960, I:435).

Therefore, because we are finite and God is infinite, the greatest possible goal we can achieve is our better understanding of the one who holds our lives in his hands. To know him is to know what is the ultimate truth and reality. To be ignorant of him is to walk in utter delusion and hopelessness. God has created this world, has ordained the entire plan of redemption, and governs this world for the chief purpose of displaying his nature to his creatures. And it is his revealed will that in seeing him we would love him and submit ourselves fully to him. With this as a foundation we can now turn to the specific question, Why does God allow Satan to work miracles?

The Reason for Satanic Miracles

If our premise is correct, then we would expect to find the Scriptures declaring that satanic miracles occur, as far as God is concerned, for the manifestation of his divine attributes, that is, to glorify himself. Satan, of course, seeks to deceive and to destroy men's souls by them. In this end he can proceed no further than God has ordained.

Exodus 7–12

This is the account of the amazing confrontation between Moses and the magicians and sorcerers of Egypt. It is, admittedly, one of the most difficult biblical passages to cogently explain. Indeed, there are things here that we do not fully comprehend. What we do know is that the evil wonderworkers were permitted by God to almost duplicate the first miracles of Moses. Why did God allow them any success when in competition against the truth? It must have been a severe trial to both Moses and the children of Israel to see Pharaoh's sorcerers competing with almost equal success.

When we bring our understanding of God's plan to manifest his nature through all that he has ordained, then we better understand this providence. It was John Calvin who referred to this class of satanic miracles as God's "last thunderbolt" (Calvin 1984, II:A:149). They occur only when he has decreed awful judgment upon a people. With the demonic imposter's amazing exhibitions of power, God allows them to further blind the minds of hardened sinners. This is exactly what Paul declares about Satan: "In whom the god of this world hath blinded the minds of them which believe not, lest the light of the glorious gospel of Christ, who is the image of God, should shine unto them" (2 Cor. 4:4).

There are times when the line of God's patience is crossed, when the cup of his wrath is filled. There comes a time when it is simply too late (see Psalm 7:11–13; Prov. 1:24–31; Isa. 55:6; Rom. 1:18, 24, 25). At such times prayer avails not (Jer. 7:16; 14:11), even the united prayers of a Moses and a Samuel (Jer. 15:1). God has decided to glorify himself by baring the arm of his power in acts of judgment. An understanding of God's infinite justice causes a "fear of the LORD." This reverential fear is foundational to basic Christian living (Prov. 1:7; 16:6; Heb. 12:28), is commanded by Christ (Matt. 10:28) and his apostles (Phil. 2:12; 1 Peter 1:17), and leads to selfless service to imperiled sinners (2 Cor. 5:10). It is good that we know of God's justice.

God's wrath fell on Pharaoh and Egypt, who cruelly oppressed his people and refused to submit to his will. God allowed their sorcerers to perform enough "counter-miracles" so that it wasn't always absolutely clear who represented the more powerful religion. Yes, there were tokens along the way that evinced the superiority of the God of Moses. When Aaron's rod swallowed up the magicians' rods (Exod. 7:12), and when the magicians could not duplicate Moses' miracles (8:18; 9:11; etc.). This was enough to assure God's people of Moses' authenticity, but was not enough to convince Pharaoh that he should flee to the God of Israel. So God accomplished the goals of maturing his people's faith through the test and of revealing his awesome retributive justice on the impenitent.

Thus, sometimes God's infinitely wise plan calls for the clear and awesome exhibition of his justice. He is a just God. That is why there is a hell. He is an infinitely holy God. That is why there is a lake of fire in which shall be punished forever "the fearful, and unbelieving, and the abominable, and murderers, . . . and sorcerers, and idolaters" (Rev. 21:8). When God caused the earth to engulf the rebellious Israelites, his power and justice were glorified (Num. 16:28–33). Through the just punishment of Pharaoh's sins, God also revealed his power and justice (Exod. 9:16; Rom. 9:16, 22). In the light of these facts we can only bow our hearts and thank him for the grace and mercy poured out on us.

The divine justice and holiness of God are not to be trifled with. We are warned, "Follow peace with all men, and holiness, without which no man shall see the Lord: . . . For our God is a consuming fire" (Heb. 12:14, 29).

The immediate execution of God's justice in this life is termed "his strange work" and "his strange act" by Isaiah (28:21). Though he may visit the iniquity of fathers on children for three and four generations, he also shows mercy to thousands of generations of those that love him and keep his commandments (Exod. 20:5, 6). This whole text shows that he is much more given to the expression of his mercy than he is to the expression of his wrath and justice. The weeping prophet affirmed, "But though he cause grief, yet will he have compassion according to the multitude of his mercies. For he doth not afflict willingly nor grieve the children of men" (Lam. 3:32, 33).

2 Thessalonians 2

The spiritual warfare waged between Moses and his opponents in the nation of Egypt is only an introduction to the trials that are to come upon the whole earth during the prophesied reign of the Antichrist. It is evident that the Scriptures here reveal that satanic miracles are permitted as a sure road leading to divine judgment.

> And then shall that Wicked be revealed, whom the Lord shall consume with the spirit of his mouth, and shall destroy with the brightness of his coming: even him, whose coming is after the working of Satan with all power and signs and lying wonders, and with all deceivableness of unrighteousness in them that perish; because they received not the love of the truth, that they might be saved. And for this cause God shall send them strong delusion, that they should believe a lie: that they all might be damned who believed not the truth, but had pleasure in unrighteousness (vv. 8–12).

The day is coming when miracles again will abound in this world. Many of them will be satanic in origin and designed by the devil to deceive. The victims of this enormous delusion will be those that "received not the love of the truth" but who "had pleasure in unrighteousness." Our hearts truly grieve over the reality of this nearly universal apostasy. The seeds of it are clearly being sown in our day. They are being watered by ignorance of Scripture, tendency toward mysticism (subjective experiences and miracle mania), and a cheapened form of the gospel, which are all present in professing Christendom. Peter warns: "For the time is come that judgment must begin at the house of God: and if it first begin at us, what shall the end be of them that obey not the gospel of God? And if the righteous scarcely be saved, where shall the ungodly and the sinner appear?" (1 Peter 4:17, 18).

To help safeguard us from misunderstanding God's nature and actions, I recommend the following comments by William Hendriksen:

> God is love. He is not a cruel monster who deliberately and with inward delight prepares people for everlasting damnation. On the contrary, he earnestly warns, proclaims the gospel, and states what will happen if people believe, also what will happen if they do not believe. He even *urges* them to accept the love for the truth. But when people, of their own accord and after repeated threats and promises, reject him and spurn his messages, then—and not until then—he hardens them . . . .
>
> When Pharaoh hardens his heart (Ex. 7:14; 8:15, 32; 9:7), God hardens Pharaoh's heart (Ex. 9:12). When the king of Israel hates God's true prophets, then the Lord permits him to be deceived by . . . a lying spirit in the mouth of other prophets (2 Chron. 18:22). When men practice impurity, God gives them up in the lusts of their hearts to impurity (Rom. 1:24, 26). And when they stubbornly refuse to acknowledge God, he finally gives them up to a base mind and to unclean behavior (Hendriksen 1955, 185, 186).

Deuteronomy 13

This passage clearly reveals the manner in which God turns satanic miracles to accomplish good. They are allowed as a severe trial to test and prove the faith of true believers. "Thou shalt not hearken unto the words of that prophet, . . . for the LORD your God proveth you, to know whether ye love the LORD your God with all your heart and with all your soul" (v. 3). Calvin remarks:

> He designedly brings the truly pious to the proof, in order to distinguish them from the hypocrites; and this takes place, when they constantly persevere in the true faith against the assaults of their temptations, and do not fall from standing. The Apostle declares the same thing also with regard to heresies, that they must needs arise in the Church "that they which are approved may be made manifest." (1 Cor. 11:19) (Calvin 1984, II:A:445).

Why does God permit satanic miracles? It is for the further manifestation of his glory. His truth is thereby magnified even higher than his power, for the word is more important than miracles (Psalm 138:2; Luke 16:31; Acts 20:32). His grace is seen in preserving the elect (Matt. 24:24), and his justice is revealed in punishing the obstinate. As Calvin concludes: "Imposters in their working of miracles are the ministers of God's vengeance, in order that the reprobate may be taken in their snares" (Calvin 1984, II:A:443).

As we continue down the path of history, drawing closer and closer to the great apocalyptic events of the last days, let us stand on the truth of God's Word. And we must keep our eyes on Christ, not on any man, lest we be turned away from him, remembering that he said, "For there shall arise false Christs, and false prophets, and shall shew great signs and wonders; insomuch that, if it were possible, they shall deceive the very elect" (Matt. 24:24). We will end this chapter with Calvin's apt remarks:

Christ warns them that false prophets will come prepared with no ordinary instruments of deception, with signs and wonders fitted to confound weak minds. For since it is by miracles that God attests the presence of his power, and since they are therefore seals of the true doctrine, we need not wonder if imposters gain credit by them. By this kind of delusion God revenges the ingratitude of men, that they who rejected the truth may believe a lie, and that they who shut their eyes against the light which was offered to them may be plunged deeper and deeper in darkness. He exercises, at the same time, the constancy of his followers, which comes to shine with greater brightness, when they give way to no kind of impostures (Calvin 1984, XVII:A:140).

3

Defeating Demons and Discerning True Faith

11

What Is
Spiritual Warfare

?

War is brutal. Its very name produces thoughts of destruction, death, sorrow, pain, and irreparable loss. Loved ones are separated; plans are postponed. Factories are converted from normal functions to producing everything necessary to win the conflict. Vacations, rest and relaxation are all sacrificed during war. Attention is riveted on defending and preserving the basic freedoms and necessities of life which are cherished. During war, survival becomes a common concern.

Who would go to war if it were not necessary? Who would choose the foxhole over the easy chair or the clash of enemies over the embrace of loved ones? Certainly no rational human being would prefer wartime to peacetime. But sometimes there is no option but war. At times individuals and nations become obsessed with the spirit of aggression or revenge. They become bent on conquering others. And otherwise peace-loving individuals are forced, for the survival of their own freedom and lives, to pick up arms and defend themselves. In such cases many people view warfare as a duty. However, there are always others who choose either to run from or to submit to the opponent. They would rather bear the consequences of retreat or defeat than pay the price of war. Certainly the issues of warfare reveal much about the character and conscience of individuals.

The Christian Soldier's Enemy

Warfare is not only a physical reality, it is also a spiritual reality. It is a fact that the Christian cannot overlook with impunity. The enemy is around us and within us. Satan and his demonic hosts are constantly poised for an attack on God's children. The devil is a murderer (John 8:44) who seeks to devour whomever he can (1 Peter 5:8). As the "prince of devils" (Matt. 9:34), the "prince of the power of the air" (Eph. 2:2), Satan directs "his angels" (Matt. 25:41) in fierce opposition to the kingdom of God.

The great weapon that Satan employs in his attacks is sin in all its forms. The sinful nature of every human being, Christian and non-Christian, leans toward obeying his commands and suggestions (Matt. 16:23). Unbelievers are his helpless captives (2 Tim. 2:26). And countless malevolent spirits are at his immediate disposal. The devil assembles the world, the flesh, and his demonic forces in constant opposition to the things of God.

Christians are enlisted into this warfare immediately upon entering the kingdom of God. The Bible is their survival manual. It presents an entirely new way of life (world view), which believers must embrace. Basic training involves becoming disciplined in spiritual perception. Believers must understand who the enemy is and what are the enemy's tactics. They must understand what are their own strengths and weaknesses. Jesus is their captain (Heb. 2:10; Josh. 5:14, 15), to whom Christians are to look for the supply of everything concerning the conflict (Heb. 12:2; John 15:5). Without such basic training Christians are left to learn by experience. And that can be deadly in warfare. Too few pastors include spiritual warfare in their discipling courses. It is no wonder that the enemy has almost free course within our ranks.

The Christian Soldier's Armor

Paul states that the nature of our battle is spiritual, not physical (Eph. 6:12). Therefore, its weapons also are not physical, but spiritual (2 Cor. 10:3, 4). It is as foolish for a soldier to oppose a squadron of bombers with a sword as it is for the Christian to fight against spiritual enemies with dependence upon human wisdom or strength. Only the spiritual armor that God has provided is sufficient for victory in these battles (Eph. 6:10–18). Charles Hodge explains:

> This divine armor is necessary to enable us to stand against the wiles of the devil. If our adversary were a man, and possessed nothing beyond human strength, ingenuity, and cunning, we might defend ourselves by human means. . . . If Satan and satanic influence are fables or figures, then all the rest of the representation concerning the spiritual conflict are empty metaphor. But if one part of this representation is literally true, the other has a corresponding depth and reality of meaning. If Satan is really the prince of the powers of darkness, ruler and god of this world; if he is the author of physical and moral evil; the great enemy of God, of Christ, and of his people, full of cunning and malice; if he is constantly seeking whom he may destroy, seducing to evil and skeptical thoughts; if all this is true, then to be ignorant of it, or to deny it, or to enter on this conflict as though it were merely a struggle between the good and bad principles in our own hearts, is to rush blindfold to destruction (C. Hodge 1982, 376, 377).

Paul declared that if he were "ignorant of Satan's devices," the devil could "get an advantage" in the conflict (2 Cor. 2:11). He knew that the evil tempter could subtly seduce the Thessalonian Christians and practically nullify his labors among them (1 Thess. 3:5). Jesus warned that Satan thus attempted to oppose the teaching of the Word and to remove it from the hearts of men (Matt. 13:19). The evil one hates the truth of Scripture because by it he is defeated (Eph. 6:17; Heb. 4:12; Jer. 23:28, 29). So, faith in the promise of God's Word neutralizes Satan's efforts against us (Eph. 6:16; 1 Peter 5:8, 9).

The Christian Soldier's Victory

The Bible declares that Jesus Christ has already defeated Satan and delivered Christians from his bondage:

> Forasmuch then as the children are partakers of flesh and blood, he also himself likewise took part of the same; that through death he might destroy him that had the power of death, that is, the devil; and deliver them who through fear of death were all their lifetime subject to bondage (Heb. 2:14, 15; also Col. 1:13).

When Christ arose and ascended, he revealed his victory over Satan, taking as his own booty those whom the devil had captured—the spoils of his glorious victory over sin, death, and hell (Col. 2:15; Matt. 12:29). The victory of Jesus Christ is the victory of all who are saved by faith in him. Hence, Satan has no legitimate authority over Christians. Whatever influence he enjoys in our lives is the result of our yielding to him in some way. Whenever Christians are tempted by him, they are commanded: "Submit yourselves therefore to God. Resist the devil, and he will flee from you" (James 4:7). This is the law of God, and Satan cannot resist it. In this manner the God of peace bruises Satan under the feet of his children (Rom. 16:20).

When Christians claim their status as God's children, through the person and work of Christ, Satan's influence over them is immediately vanquished. This fact is of greatest practical value to the everyday life of the believer. Evil thoughts that Satan suggests to our minds stick and burn like fiery darts, until opposed by the living faith of the Christian (Eph. 6:16). A day's activities proceed without demonic hindrance for believers who continually submit their minds and plans to the Lord

(Prov. 3:5, 6; 1 John 5:18). Christians' personal lives, families, businesses, churches, and communities can all be positively influenced by this aggressive spiritual warfare.

The Christian Soldier's Dilemma

But what happens when believers refuse to partake in this spiritual battle, when they neglect to "put on the whole armor of God, that ye may be able to stand against the wiles of the devil" (Eph. 6:11)? Well, the sad truth is that such Christians do not stand. They waver, falter, and are often defeated by the enemy. Instead of routing the devil, they open the door for Satan, giving him unnecessary influence in their lives (Eph. 4:27).

Such are like Peter, to whom Jesus said, "Why sleep ye? rise and pray, lest ye enter into temptation" (Luke 22:46). Instead of praying, Peter responded physically to the enemy (John 18:10), was rebuked by Christ (Matt. 26:52, 53), then forsook the Lord and later denied him. Satan was behind all this; but, he did not succeed in totally defeating Peter, because Jesus prayed that Peter's faith would not fail (Luke 22:31, 32). Jesus engaged in spiritual warfare against Satan in behalf of Peter. How thankful we should be that we also "have an advocate with the Father, Jesus Christ the righteous" (1 John 2:1). The praise of Jeremiah daily belongs on every Christian's lips: "It is of the LORD's mercies that we are not consumed, because his compassions fail not. They are new every morning: great is thy faithfulness" (Lam. 3:22, 23).

Warfare is not fun and games. For Christians spiritual warfare is a dangerous and demanding duty. Although they may have profound assurance of their salvation (John 10:28), believers must realize that they are called to lives of sacrifice and service. Salvation is all of grace. And God promises to supply for every true believer the grace to persevere in this spiritual warfare (Job 17:9; Prov. 4:18; Mark 13:13; Phil. 2:12). Archibald Alexander states:

From this passage (Eph. 6:12) it is evident that our spiritual foes are numerous and powerful, and that the believer's conflict with them is violent: it is a 'wrestling,' or a contention which requires them to put forth all their strength, and to exercise all their skill (A. Alexander 1967, 153).

Spiritual warfare, when performed for others, is likened to the travail of a mother when giving birth to her child (Gal. 4:19). There is nothing easy about such travail. But what mother, when afterward holding her sweet child, claims that the baby is not worth the travail? Though demanding sacrifice, spiritual warfare is well worth the cost, also.

The Christian Soldier's Warfare: Prayer

Spiritual warfare is primarily aggressive prayer (Eph. 6:18). It can be wrought for oneself (Luke 22:40; 1 Peter 5:6–9; Jude 20, 21) or for others (Rom. 15:30; 2 Cor. 1:10, 11). Paul explained how Epaphras entered into regular, spiritual warfare in behalf of the Colossians by "laboring fervently for you in prayers, that ye may stand perfect and complete in all the will of God" (Col. 4:12). To labor fervently for another demands sacrifice. As self-centeredness abounds today, it is no wonder that so few are laboring in this manner for others. Nevertheless, Ephesians 6:18 commands all Christians to war in prayer for each other. Hodge remarks:

> The conflict of which the apostle has been speaking is not merely a single combat between the individual and the powers of darkness. No soldier entering battle prays for himself, alone, but for all his fellow soldiers also. They form one army, and the success of one is the success of all. In like manner Christians are united as one army, and therefore have a common cause; and each must pray for all (C. Hodge 1982, 392).

True spiritual warfare, then, is not an avocation, but rather, an arduous struggle. The fact that so few are engaged in this battle betrays the unbelieving and selfish character of today's Christianity. Spiritual retreat and defeat have become the rule instead of the exception. Imperceptible to the vast advances being made by Satan's kingdom, lazy Christians will sit in the comforts of their own homes thinking all is safe. Few seem to take seriously the danger to which they are constantly exposed by the world, the flesh, and the devil. The command to "pray without ceasing" (1 Thess. 5:17) or to "walk with God" (Gen. 5:22–24; 6:9; 17:1) seems to many modern Christians to be as impossible to achieve as it is unnecessary to follow. Alexander warned:

> Christians are more injured in this warfare by the insidious and secret influence of their enemies lulling them into the sleep of carnal security, than by all their open and violent assaults. No duty is more necessary, in maintaining this conflict, than watchfulness. Unceasing vigilance is indispensible. "Watch and pray that ye enter not into temptation"—"and what I say unto you, I say unto all, Watch" (A. Alexander 1967, 127).

The Christian Soldier's Warfare: Power Encounter

To many Christians in "deliverance ministries" spiritual warfare is synonymous with power encounter. Confronting and casting out demons from the demonized is their chief concern. Most of the current literature on spiritual warfare focuses mainly on exorcism. I think this is an unhealthy and imbalanced approach to spiritual warfare. It is simply unbiblical. The inspired teaching of Paul mentions prayer much, but exorcism little. The epistles were written to help guide Christian church members in their everyday life. Prayer is the norm of spiritual warfare; exorcism is the exception.

Although power encounter with the demonic is a legitimate aspect of the Christian's spiritual warfare, it is only a very small part. More often than not, when this sphere is advanced as the center of one's concentration, an unhealthy spirit of oppression and extremism occurs. Demons are seen in almost everything and nearly everyone. The Christian is driven by presumption, calling it discernment. Exorcising demons from people, rooms, objects is seen as the secret of spiritual progress. The end result seems to be that the Christian becomes more demon conscious than God conscious, thereby performing exactly what Satan desires. While professing Christ's power and lordship, this type of Christian is actually denying it by centering his life, mind, and activity on the power and activity of Satan.

The devil loves extremes. One cannot be balanced and extreme at the same time. Stability comes by understanding and following Scripture (Isa. 33:6). Therefore, the devil constantly attempts to jar the Christian's balance by urging him or her to pursue some tangent. Imbalance in any direction is the aim of Satan. Some deny the reality of demonization, which is one extreme, whereas others follow the opposite extreme by becoming obsessed with demonic activities. Timothy Warner, while carrying on a demanding deliverance ministry, wisely counsels: "I do not suggest that missionaries go on a 'lion' hunt trying to set up a series of dramatic power encounters. But neither do I suggest that we back off in fear when the power and glory of God are being challenged by men under the power of demons" (Warner 1986, 70).

Miracle or Magic?

Why include a chapter on spiritual warfare in a book on miracles, you might ask? Because the exorcisms by Christ and his apostles were true miracles. They were wrought by "the finger of God" (Luke 11:20), that is by "the Spirit of God" (Matt. 12:28). When John saw a man casting out demons in Christ's name, he told the man to stop. Jesus responded, "Forbid him not: for there is no man which shall do a miracle in my name, that can lightly [quickly thereafter] speak evil of me" (Mark 9:38, 39). Jesus there affirmed that true miracles were wrought by God's power when his children cast out demons in his name. Miracles performed by God do not fail. Miracles truly wrought in the name of Christ did not fail.

Professed exorcisms that fall short of complete deliverance are not miracles and therefore are not the works of God. Is the deliverance that God works known by the evidences of limitation, frailty, confusion, impotence and re-invasion? Never! But this type of "deliverance" abounds today both inside and outside Christianity. Where in our inspired guidebook, the Bible, do we see Christians struggling for hours with demons who refuse to be cast out? Where are there examples of true exorcism that led to almost immediate re-invasion by demons? Where is there a single example of a born again believer being delivered of inhabiting demons? We are told, though, that all of these phenomena are regular occurrences in the ministries of today's deliverance ministers. (See appendix 5, "Can Christians be Demon-Possessed?")

There were Jewish exorcists in the first century (Acts 19:13; Luke 11:19). They were amazed at the contrast between their elaborate, ritualistic exorcisms and the technique of Jesus, who cast out demons with a word and was invariably obeyed. They defended themselves by declaring that Jesus cast out demons through the power of Satan (Matt. 12:25–32).

I do not like the trend toward ritualistic exorcisms that is increasing in our day. The concept of proper wording and surroundings is appearing in some Christian how-to-do-it manuals on casting out demons. When success in deliverance ministries centers on saying the right words or being in the right environment, the whole procedure dangerously approaches magic. One author notes:

> Christ's disciples cast out demons "in the name of Jesus" (Mark 16:17; Luke 10:17). The name stands for the infinite Person behind the name, and does not contain any magical power in itself. When prostituted into a ritualistic rigmarole, however, as in white magic, it becomes a deceiving tool in the hands of Satan's agents to delude the undiscerning by false miracles and spurious healings. Such diabolical miracles do

not destroy Satan's kingdom, but build it up. Diabolical exorcism does not produce true dispossession, but a mere re-allocation (of demons). Demonic healing may relieve physical symptoms, but substitute a psychical ill or doctrinal form of error. This subterfuge explains in part the increase of theological decadence and phenomenal growth of sects and cults within professing Christianity in these latter days (Unger 1985, 120).

Testing the Spirits

In much present-day Christian exorcism there is a remarkable amount of dialogue with demons. This is in sharp contrast with the example of Christ, who often demanded their silence (Mark 1:34; Luke 4:41). This practice is also interesting in the light of biblical commands not to have anything to do with evil spirits or their mediums (see Lev. 19:31; 20:6; 1 Sam. 28:3; 2 Kings 21:6; 23:24; Isa. 8:19, 20). God's Word clearly reproves the "consulter with familiar spirits" (Deut. 18:10, 11). And Paul warns of the "[departure] from the faith" which is to occur "in the latter times" because of some "giving heed to seducing spirits" (1 Tim. 4:1).

Why then do Christians in deliverance ministries communicate so extensively with the inhabiting demons? Most practitioners would justify their discourse with demons from the command of John to "try [test] the spirits" (1 John 4:1). Indeed, they interpret that passage as a command to thus communicate with demons. But the test that John advances is a doctrinal test that the Christian is to apply to the false prophet mentioned in verse one. This text has nothing to do with addressing demons. Testing the spirits is testing the hearts of the false prophets by closely examining their doctrine. John said, "We [apostles] are of God: he that knoweth God heareth us; he that is not of God heareth not us. Hereby know we the spirit of truth, and the spirit of error" (1 John 4:6). The test to be utilized by the discerning Christian is the Word of God applied to the teachings of all persons.

Even though they have no biblical parallel, most deliverance ministers are blind to this practice of conversing with demons. Some affirm that the statements made by demons are trustworthy when correctly tested. And the Christian exorcist bases the entire deliverance upon the information supplied by the demons. Demons are "called up," "sent down," "bound," and "cast into the abyss" by the multiplied hundreds. Needless to say, this procedure often takes hours and sometimes even days. And all the time the deliverer is acting upon information given by deceptive spirits.

How can demons be trusted? The Bible, when describing Satan, declares, "there is no truth in him" (John 8:44). Even deliverance advocates admit that the test for truth they apply to the demons' statements "is not a 100% safeguard, and double checking is recommended because evil spirits are very intelligent and deceitful" (Ensign and Howe 1984, 171). If demons can slip in some erroneous statements, who is to judge what is true and what is false? This is all very dangerous ground, as it goes far beyond the simplicity and power of biblical practice.

I believe that God still works miracles through his children. But I object to the claim that the supernatural gifts exist today, from chiefly two standpoints. First, the conferring of miraculous gifts always accompanied the ministry of an apostle as one of the "signs of an apostle" (2 Cor. 12:12). Since there are no more apostles, there can be no more miraculous gifts (see chapters 4, 5, and 6). Second, there is no conclusive evidence that the alleged gifts of our day match the truly miraculous gifts of the New Testament era (see chapter 7).

However, the practice of casting out demons is never specifically mentioned as a miraculous gift of the Holy Spirit. Gifts were used regularly and often. The miraculous expulsion of demons in Jesus' name is the birthright of every child of God. But, like all miracles, exorcism is not the normal everyday experience. It is evident that Christians all over the world are casting out demons in the name of Christ. And why should this be thought strange? What great glory is given to God when one of his creatures is liberated from the enslaving power of Satan;

what evidence is given to the whole community that "greater is He that is in you, than he that is in the world" (1 John 4:4). At times such power encounters lead directly to large numbers coming to Christ.

Even though clear power encounters occur but rarely in the normal Christian's life, we should not be ignorant of this part of our warfare. There is an unquestionable increase of overt demonic activity everywhere, especially in the Western world. The more direct becomes the confrontation between the kingdom of God and the kingdom of Satan, the more likely it is that such power encounters will occur. The Christian should not back away from the spiritual warfare, for this would dishonor Almighty God by acquiescing to the usurping power of the devil. Simple, childlike faith in what Christ has accomplished for us and in the armor he has provided for us is sufficient to win the day.

Christians serve a God of power, infinite power. He is also amazingly patient. Sometimes it is not his will to exert his power and displace or defeat the enemy. Paul learned this, and so must we (2 Cor. 12:8, 9). Sometimes it is even God's will that his children lose a battle or a power encounter. The two prophets of Revelation 11 were opposed and slain by the beast (v. 7). They lost to the beast, and the whole world rejoiced at their defeat (vv. 9, 10), being further convinced that darkness is light (13:4). And when the prophets were raised from the dead, "great fear fell upon them which saw them" (11:11). Also, John records, "And it was given unto him to make war with the saints, and to overcome them" (13:7). So it behooves us not to develop a power encounter mania and make it the norm for our evangelism. Power evangelism proponents should ponder this carefully. Let's remember that God is sovereign. No one directs him in his work. He is not on the end of a rope, always to appear when we give a sudden yank. We shouldn't put him on the spot by power encounters of our own making. If we will wait for those that he arranges, we will probably have more than enough.

God is glorified every time sin is vanquished. Satan is thereby thwarted. Power encounters need not be dramatic. They do not have to involve the demonized, though at times they may. Whenever a fiery arrow of satanic temptation has been discerned and extinguished from our minds, a successful power encounter has occurred, and the glorious power of the risen Christ has been manifested. Whenever the intercession of a concerned Christian is poured out for another needy person, spiritual warfare is engaged in. Therefore, Satan's efforts are not to be seen in only the overt form of demonization. He may be as much behind an argument between two Christians as he is in a seance. Error is as much his child as is the occult. So the reproof of error, in the spirit of Christian love, may be a successful power encounter.

Satan is near, and his deceptive powers are great. He is continually waging vehement war through the flesh, unbelievers, and demons. The believer has no hope for victory if he depends on his own strength and power. But, our personal union with the risen Christ can bring victory on all fronts, and will certainly achieve full and complete victory eventually. So let us be vigilant and aggressive in every aspect of our spiritual warfare, for this is the will of God.

12

Saving Faith
or the Experience
of Demons

?

Demons will not be saved. On this point all Christians agree. With this as a foundation, we can develop an understanding of the nature of saving faith that is sorely needed by the church today. The statements and characteristics of demons, as recorded in the New Testament, aid us in this important study.

Biblical writers have recorded several demonic "professions of faith." Evangelicals will agree that the statements made by those condemned spirits cannot be legitimate proofs of their possessing saving faith. The danger today is this: there are many whose assurance of salvation is based on nothing more than a single expression of faith. As we study the demons' statements it will become clear that some professions of faith today bear a remarkable resemblance to those made by demons. If this is the case, then such statements are inadequate in themselves to prove one's salvation. And those hoping that such will save them may be in grave peril.

124

Demonic Faith

This line of reasoning concerning salvation is nothing new. James used it in his epistle when exposing the counterfeit faith threatening the church in his day. He wrote, "Thou believest that God is one; thou doest well: the demons also believe, and shudder" (James 2:19 ASV).

James revealed that not all faith is saving faith. The word for faith in the New Testament is the same word for belief. To believe, then, is the same as to have faith. So, faith is not an exclusively Christian word, but is used of demons and unbelievers as well as by Christians. There are different types of faith, some of which cannot save from sin.

Historic Faith

The demons believe. This is a fact declared by God. Their belief or faith is an historic faith. They believe the facts of history, including the history of redemption. They know that God exists and rules, and that they cannot overthrow him. They know that Jesus died and rose from the dead. This historic faith does not change their eternal destiny. And James argued that such a faith would not save a human soul, either. His whole argument in this passage (2:14–26) is that no faith is saving faith that is not a living faith, a productive faith—what Paul called a "faith which worketh by love" (Gal. 5:6). A faith that affects only the mind is purely historical. Such a solitary faith stands naked, unclothed by transforming power and grace. Such a faith the demons have, and it cannot save.

Demonic Statements of Faith

In Mark 5:6, 7 a remarkable text is recorded. It sheds some interesting light on demonic beliefs: "And when he saw Jesus from afar, he ran and worshipped him; and crying out with a loud voice, he saith, What have I to do with thee, Jesus, thou Son of the Most High God? I adjure thee by God, torment me not" (ASV; see also Luke 8:26ff; Matt. 8:28ff).

A demon worshiping? Yes, and also attesting that this man in front of him was the very Son of God, thereby asserting faith in Jesus' deity. He also recognized that this Jesus had the power to punish him, and therefore the demon feared him.

It is amazing what a demon will say when faced by his Creator. Insincere homage is rendered because he is scared to death. He selfishly seeks mercy, realizing his danger. Thus he utters a few Christ-honoring statements in an attempt to pacify God and escape his certain doom for a while longer.

How many people today profess faith in Christ because they are momentarily impressed with the danger of their sin-laden lives, and fear the possibility of death? How many times have such cries for mercy arisen from men in battle and from the sick in hospitals? And often all is forgotten when the danger has passed. They return to their sinful ways just as certainly as the demons returned to their terrorism. We thank God that there are some exceptions, such as the thief on the cross who sincerely repented, trusting in Christ as his personal Savior (Luke 23:39–43).

Another glimpse into the demonic mind is granted us in Luke 4:34. There the demon asserts: "What have we to do with thee, thou Jesus of Nazareth? art thou come to destroy us? I know thee who thou art; the Holy One of God" (also Mark 1:23ff).

Demons are familiar with the facts of history and redemption. They knew that Jesus came out of Nazareth. In this instance it was recognized that Jesus was the Messiah, the Anointed One promised and sent by God. The demons professed much more than did the Pharisees, the religious leaders of that day. The demonic spokesman even highlighted God's holiness. How astounding—these creatures of darkness speaking of God's holiness! Yet none of this saved them. An historic faith is capable of producing any number of like professions in us, too, without making us the children of God.

The most amazing revelation of demonic faith is seen in Acts 16:17. Paul and Silas had a very strange companion in their evangelism—a demonized sorceress. Luke here records: "The same followed Paul and us, and cried, saying, These men are the servants of the most high God, which shew unto us the way of salvation." The demon saw no problem with honoring the servants of God. Nor was it out of the question for a demon to urge his servant to proclaim where the way of salvation might be found. This the woman did repeatedly, day after day. Paul was "grieved" by her assistance and exorcised the demon from her in the name of Jesus Christ (v. 18).

It is hard to conceive of a demon-possessed woman evangelizing, isn't it? We picture demons as uttering only loathsome blasphemies. They, too, love to become angels of light so they can later deceive. Is it possible for an unbeliever to witness for Christ? Yes, it is. An historical faith can be so strong that its possessor wants to share his or her beliefs with others. Both Judas Iscariot and Demas probably led many to God before they apostasized (Luke 9:1–6; Col. 4:14; 2 Tim. 4:10).

As we combine our biblical evidence and draw conclusions, we do so realizing the deep seriousness of our topic. It is important that Christians have assurance of their salvation. It is likewise important that such assurance be well-founded on legitimate, biblical evidence. Our study proves that no verbal profession of faith, however extensive, is a sure evidence of salvation if standing alone. We may also deduce that outward forms of worship and service may all be counterfeited and hence cannot be ample proofs of one's spiritual status (see Matt. 7:21–23).

Temporary Faith

Some teach that once a person has made a profession of faith, nothing should ever be said or done to make that person question or doubt his or her salvation. Paul did not follow such a practice. He cautioned the Corinthians, "Examine yourselves, whether ye be in the faith; prove your own selves" (2 Cor. 13:5). The reason for this is evident when we consider what Jesus taught in the parable of the sower and the seed (Matt. 13:3–23). Jesus there explains that it is not the mere hearer of the Word who is saved (v. 19). Neither is saving faith present in the life of everyone who receives the message of the Word "with joy" (vv. 20, 21). Luke records it as follows: "They on the rock are they, which, when they hear, receive the word with joy; and these have no root, which for a while *believe,* and in time of temptation fall away" (Luke 8:13, italics added).

Notice that some believe for a while. This is temporary faith. It is not saving faith, though at first it resembles true saving faith. Elsewhere Jesus spoke to "those Jews which believed on him" and called them the children of the devil (John 8:30–44). It is possible to listen to the gospel attentively and respond in a positive manner without truly being born again.

Jesus even states that a person might be temporarily fruitful after a profession of faith without truly being a child of God (Matt. 13:22). The person might make certain changes and develop new discipline; however, the cares of and lusts for things of this world eventually strangle the good intentions, leaving the person bound to his or her evil nature. Judas and Demas are perhaps examples of this type of believer (see also John 12:42, 43; 1 Cor. 15:2).

Biblical Use of the Word *Saved*

The Bible speaks of salvation in two different ways. It speaks of eternal life being given to those who have received the Son of God into their lives as Lord and Savior by faith (John 1:12; 3:36; 5:24; Rom. 10:9; Eph. 2:8, 9; 1 John 5:11, 12). But it also speaks of salvation as following a lifetime of faith and struggle. As in the following verses:

> And ye shall be hated of all men for my name's sake: but he that shall endure unto the end, the same shall be saved (Mark 13:13).
>
> Strive to enter in at the strait gate: for many, I say unto you, will seek to enter in, and shall not be able (Luke 13:24).

Then said Jesus unto his disciples, If any man will come after me, let him deny himself, and take up his cross, and follow me. For whosoever will save his life shall lose it: and whosoever will lose his life for my sake shall find it. For what is a man profited, if he shall gain the whole world, and lose his own soul? or what shall a man give in exchange for his soul? (Matt. 16:24–26).

Paul cautioned professing Christians to "work out [their] own salvation with fear and trembling" (Phil. 2:12). He also warned, "Wherefore let him that thinketh he standeth take heed lest he fall" (1 Cor. 10:12). And Peter spoke of "receiving the end of your faith, even the salvation of your souls" (1 Peter 1:9). Almost all the stress today is on *the beginning* of one's faith, on conversion. But this was not the stress of Peter and Paul. Peter taught that all Christians "are kept by the power of God through faith unto salvation ready to be revealed in the last time" (1 Peter 1:5). Christian perseverance is a great evidence of the possession of saving faith.

So, Christians are saved when they are converted. And they are saved when the last vestige of sin is removed from their lives. Both of these representations of salvation, of course, are true. They are both taught clearly in God's Word. The concept of salvation in the Bible involves the believer's entire existence. Romans 8:30 views the whole spectrum of salvation: "Moreover whom he did predestinate, them he also called: and whom he called, them he also justified: and whom he justified, them he also glorified." This can be diagrammed as follows:

How God Saves Human Beings
The Christian in Romans 8:30

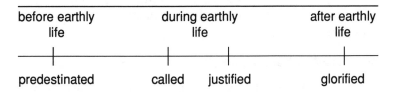

before earthly life	during earthly life		after earthly life
predestinated	called	justified	glorified

Christians are *predestinated* to salvation from eternity (Eph. 1:4, 5; 2 Thess. 2:13; 2 Tim. 1:9; Rev. 17:8; 21:27). They are *called* to the actual possession of salvation by the outward ministry of the Word (Rom. 10:14–17; 1 Peter 1:23) accompanied by the inward enabling of the Holy Spirit (Acts 16:14; John 6:44; Titus 3:5). This is their conversion. Based on their faith, God *justifies* them (Rom. 3:24, 28). That is, he declares them to be clothed in Christ's righteousness and thereby accepted as his children. They actually stand without guilt before his law. And Paul declares that once a person is justified by God, he cannot be condemned or lose his salvation (Rom. 8:1, 32, 33). Nevertheless, salvation is not completed until the Christian is perfected or *glorified* in God's presence. And this occurs at the end of the believer's life on earth (1 John 3:2; John 17:24; Rev. 21:3, 4).

People are considered saved when they are called and justified by God. However, from all that we have seen from Scripture, it is extremely dangerous for us to tell people they are saved simply because they have made outward professions of faith. People's sincerity is known only to God. How they will respond to the future trials of their faith is unknown to us. We can only pray for their perseverance and attempt to guide and help their growth in grace.

We must remember that Jesus commissioned the church to make *disciples,* not *converts* (Matt 28:18–20). Our job is not done when a conversion occurs. We must earnestly nurture the convert in the Word of God. While a missionary in Africa, I regularly saw only about 15 percent of those who came forward in open-air meetings actually discipled in the Christian faith. I have no biblical reason to believe that the other 85 percent were truly converted. Yes, there are many around the globe who believe, but with something less than saving faith, and they eventually fall away.

The Proofs of Saving Faith

Paul told the Corinthians to test and prove that they were saved (2 Cor. 13:5). What are those characteristics that positively identify saving faith? They must be objective and viewable by others, because the election of others can be known (1 Thess. 1:4). Paul spoke of his fellow laborers as those "whose names are in the book of life" (Phil. 4:3). How did Paul know this? Had Paul seen the book of life? No, but he saw the evidences of saving grace manifested in their lives.

In the parable of the sower and the seed, Jesus identified the good ground (the possessor of saving faith) by three signs: hearing the message of salvation, understanding its practical implications for the individual, and a steady spiritual progress or fruitfulness (Matt. 13:23).

Many today do not understand the nature of saving faith. Jesus said that understanding the Word is essential for salvation. Historical faith involves only knowledge and belief. A person learns about Christ and accepts as true what is learned. This demands nothing from a person's life; it is all rather impersonal. But true saving faith includes knowledge, belief, *and trust*. We hear much about accepting Christ as our personal Savior. Christ does not become our Savior in a personal way if there is no trust, yielding, or commitment of ourselves to him.

Simple belief is not the only element of saving faith. Note how Paul uses the words *trusted* and *believed* interchangeably in the following verses: "That we should be to the praise of his glory, who first trusted in Christ. In whom ye also trusted, after that ye heard the word of truth, the gospel of your salvation: in whom also after that ye believed, ye were sealed with that holy Spirit of promise" (Eph. 1:12, 13).

The Westminster Confession of Faith defines saving faith as follows: "But the principal acts of saving faith are, accepting, receiving, and resting upon Christ alone for justification, sanctification, and eternal life" (chapter 14). You see, there must be a resting or trusting upon Christ. This has been the historic understanding of evangelical Christianity for centuries. The Larger Catechism answers the question, what is justifying faith?:

> Justifying faith is a saving grace, wrought in the heart of a sinner, by the Spirit and Word of God, whereby he, being con-

vinced of his sin and misery, . . . *not only assenteth to the truth of the promises of the gospel, but receiveth and resteth upon Christ* . . . for pardon of sin, and for the accepting and accounting of his person righteous in the sight of God for salvation (Larger Catechism no. 72, italics added).

The "easy believism" or cheapened gospel being offered by so many today is producing easygoing and cheap Christians. Another reason for this declension of true Christianity is the way many hardly mention, much less define, what sin is. The brave defender of the faith J. Gresham Machen (1881–1937) affirmed:

> We preachers do not preach hell enough, and we do not say enough about sin. We talk about the gospel and wonder why people are not interested in what we say. Of course they are not interested. No man is interested in a piece of good news unless he has the consciousness of needing it; no man is interested in an offer of salvation unless he knows there is something from which he needs to be saved. It is quite useless to ask a man to adopt the Christian view of the gospel unless he first has the Christian view of sin (Machen 1982, 34).

It is vital that we understand the nature of saving faith and the nature of sin if we are to rightly understand the Christian gospel.

The seed sown into good soil is characterized by both spiritual understanding and abundant fruitfulness, according to Jesus (Matt. 13:23). What is the nature of the fruitfulness that Jesus mentioned in this parable? Is it the multiplication of signs and wonders in our lives? If so, then very few will be saved. Does fruitfulness here chiefly refer to leading other people to Christ? If this is so, then only a small number of professing Christians are actually possessors of saving faith. I think that Paul well declares what type of fruit we are to look for.

The presence of the fruit of the Spirit of God is the surest proof that we have the Spirit, and hence, are truly saved. No person is a Christian who has not the Spirit of God in his or her life (Rom. 8:9; 1 Cor. 3:16; 12:13; 2 Cor. 1:22; 5:5; Eph. 1:13, 14). Paul writes: "This I say then, Walk in the Spirit, and ye shall not fulfil the lust of the flesh. . . . But the fruit of the Spirit is love, joy, peace, longsuffering, gentleness, goodness, faith, meekness, temperance: against such there is no law" (Gal. 5:16, 22, 23).

The chiefest fruit of the Spirit is love to God and to our neighbor (Matt. 22:37–40; 1 Cor. 13; Gal. 5:14; James 2:8). We show our love to Christ by keeping his commandments (John 14:21). In a free and unpersecuting land it takes very little to profess to being a Christian. Jesus asked, "And why call ye me, Lord, Lord, and do not the things which I say?" (Luke 6:46). Talk is certainly cheap. An obedient love is, however, along with the other sanctifying graces of the Spirit of God, the greatest proof of one's salvation.

The Spirit of God is best known as the Holy Spirit. He is the author and preserver of holiness within his children. Paul states that Christians "have your fruit unto holiness" (Rom. 6:22). Puritan Thomas Watson (1620–1686) wrote, "A thousand praises and doxologies do not honour God so much as the mortifying of one lust" (Watson 1970, 37).

Demons can verbalize great truths. They can pretend to assist in evangelism and can even encourage the outward worship of God. But they cannot love. They have no joy or peace, because they trust not in Christ. They are impatient and fierce rather than longsuffering, gentle, and meek. They are devoid of true goodness and faith. They are the servants of sin and know nothing of self-control. In short, they are devoid of the fruit of God's Holy Spirit.

Fruit takes time to grow, mature, and ripen. So does the fruit of the Spirit within the children of God. True faith produces more than an isolated confession, or a momentary impression. It produces a life devoted to Christ as Lord: a life which, however slowly and sporadically, makes progress in grace until it is made perfect in glory. He who has begun a good work in his children will perform it until the day of Jesus Christ (Phil. 1:6).

The difference between a man possessing saving faith and the experience of demons is that the one *receives* Christ as his own personal Savior; the other impersonally *recognizes* Christ as the Son of God. The Christian humbly *submits* to Christ as lord and master; whereas the experience of demons leads only to an empty *profession* of Christ as king. True Christianity consists of "the doctrine which is according to godliness" (1 Tim. 6:3); whereas counterfeit Christianity produces only "a form of godliness, but denying the power thereof" (2 Tim. 3:5).

In a day when hundreds of thousands of people are professing to be born again, it is crucial that they understand what the Scriptures state about the nature and effects of saving faith. Ministers ought to be leading their flocks into careful spiritual self-examination instead of advocating a cheapened and spurious form of Christian faith. Paul warned:

> Now the Spirit speaketh expressly, that in the latter times some shall depart from the faith, giving heed to seducing spirits, and doctrines of devils; . . . If thou put the brethren in remembrance of these things, thou shalt be a good minister of Jesus Christ, nourished up in the words of faith and of good doctrine, whereunto thou hast attained (1 Tim. 4:1, 6).

13

How Dangerous
Is False
Doctrine

?

Today we hear much about the need to cooperate and the importance of dialogue in the religious world. A popular cliché is "Doctrine divides, but love unites." We are told of the great progress being made in the conciliar movement. And it is no longer unusual to see renowned evangelical Christians entering into common religious causes with those who deny the most basic of biblical doctrines. Indeed, to speak against this enchanting ecumenical spirit is to hazard branding oneself as narrow-minded, old-fashioned, unloving, bigoted, fundamentalistic, or unprogressive.

But is this spirit of religious détente really progress? Is it pleasing to the Lord? C. S. Lewis aptly wrote:

> We all want progress. But progress means getting nearer to the place where you want to be. And if you have taken a wrong turning, then to go forward does not get you any nearer. If you are on the wrong road, progress means doing an about-turn

and walking back to the right road; and in that case the man who turns back soonest is the most progressive (Lewis, 1978, 36).

If God's Word advocates tolerance of false doctrine, then Christians have nothing to fear from it. And those who are reluctant to dialogue or cooperate with people holding opposite views are truly obstacles to progress. But if the Bible warns the Christian to have nothing to do with error, then the trend of our day is indeed frightening.

In his last book, Francis Schaeffer expressed alarm in this very area. He lamented:

> Here is the great evangelical disaster—the failure of the evangelical world to stand for truth as truth. There is only one word for this—accommodation: the evangelical church has accommodated to the world spirit of the age. . . .
> Truth carries with it confrontation. Truth demands confrontation; loving confrontation, but confrontation nevertheless. If our reflex action is always accommodation regardless of the centrality of the truth involved, there is something wrong (Schaeffer 1984, 37, 64).

We have seen the blinding power of satanic miracles. False doctrine also has an enormous power to blind the mind. We should remember that, whether the means be a miracle or error, Satan's chief aim is the ultimate destruction of human souls. Paul declared: "But if our gospel be hid, it is hid to them that are lost: in whom the god of this world hath blinded the minds of them which believe not, lest the light of the glorious gospel of Christ, who is the image of God, should shine unto them" (2 Cor. 4:3, 4).

The Peril of False Doctrine

Obvious Biblical Commands

God often warns against false doctrine and those who perpetuate it. As the following points will prove, this is no obscurely revealed instruction. Scripture's teaching on the danger of error is not open to question. It is unmistakably and undebatably clear: stay away from error and its teachers.

Solomon counseled: "Cease, my son, to hear the instruction that causeth to err from the words of knowledge" (Prov. 19:27). On this verse the Christian sage Thomas Scott (1747–1821) boldly declared:

> Insinuating infidels, skeptics, and ungodly men of various kinds, who endeavor to argue young persons out of their religious scruples, and excite their contempt of their pious parents or teachers, under the pretence of enlarging their minds, and freeing them from the shackles of prejudice and superstition; with all those ministers of religion, however distinguished, whose instructions are antiscriptural, or unscriptural; answer the description here given. They administer poison instead of medicine: and their books, sermons, sarcastical harangues, and corrupt conversation, should carefully be shunned more than a pestilence (Scott, 1846, vol. 2, 329).

The psalmist declares that God's blessing is on "the man that walketh not in the counsel of the ungodly, nor standeth in the way of sinners, nor sitteth in the seat of the scornful." Instead of following the errors of the men of this world, the fruitful believer puts "his delight . . . in the law of the LORD; and in his law doth he meditate day and night" (Ps. 1:1, 2).

Solomon, realizing the dangers of contact with error, commands, "Go from the presence of a foolish man, when thou perceivest not in him the lips of knowledge" (Prov. 14:7). Paul likewise states: "Now I beseech you, brethren, mark them which cause divisions and offenses contrary to the doctrine which ye have learned; and avoid them. For they that are such serve not our Lord Jesus Christ, but their own belly; and by good words and fair speeches deceive the heart of the simple" (Rom. 16:17, 18).

When teaching on these verses, Charles Hodge noted:

It is the duty of Christians to be constantly watchful over the peace and purity of the church, and not to allow those who cause divisions and scandals, by departing from true doctrines, to pursue their course unnoticed. With all such we should break off every connection which either sanctions their opinions and conduct, or gives them facilities for effecting evil (C. Hodge, 1972, 454).

One cannot fully appreciate the danger of false doctrine without understanding the stark denunciations of the Bible against false teachers, false ministers, and false prophets (see Deut. 18:20–22; Isa. 5:20; 9:14, 15; Jer. 14:13–16; 20:6; 23:1–40; Ezek. 13:1–23; 34:1–31; Hosea 4:6–10; Micah 3:5–7; Zech. 13:2–6; Mal. 2:8, 9; Matt. 5:19; 7:15–23; 15:2–20; 23:2–33; Luke 11:38–52; 2 Tim. 3:1–9; Titus 3:10, 11; James 3:1; 2 Peter 2:1–22; Jude 4–19). A perusal of just a few of these texts would highlight the deep seriousness with which God views the teachers of serious false doctrines.

False Doctrine Is Subtle

Jesus likened error to leaven (Matt 16:6, 11, 12), and told his disciples to beware of it. A little error can seep in and corrupt one's faith. Paul wondered how this could happen to the Galatians:

Ye did run well; who did hinder you that ye should not obey the truth? This persuasion cometh not of him that calleth you. A little leaven leaveneth the whole lump. . . . he that troubleth you shall bear his judgment, whosoever he be. . . . I would they were even cut off which trouble you (Gal. 5:7–10, 12).

Error works like a cancer, as Paul explained: "But shun profane and vain babblings: for they will increase unto more ungodliness. And their word will eat as doth a canker: of whom is Hymenaeus and Philetus" (2 Tim. 2:16, 17).

Our sinful nature readily accepts false doctrine, especially those forms that contain partial truths. Our hearts are corrupt and deceivable (Jer. 17:9). The "way which seemeth right unto a man" leads to "death" (Prov. 14:12). The "natural" or unregenerate man cannot understand spiritual truth without the assistance of the Holy Spirit (1 Cor. 2:14). Indeed, we are so prone to error that Solomon warned, "He that trusteth in his own heart is a fool" (Prov. 28:26). The Lord well depicted man's folly in this regard as follows: "A wonderful and horrible thing is committed in the land; the prophets prophesy falsely, . . . and my people love to have it so: and what will ye do in the end thereof?" (Jer. 5:30, 31).

It is easier now to understand why Solomon says to walk away from those who teach error. We are susceptible to believing it. Just as cancer subtly overtakes the body, so false doctrine, if not countered, can destroy one's spiritual foundation. The following command of John used to be rigidly followed: "If there come any unto you, and bring not this doctrine, receive him not into your house, neither bid him God speed (Good day): for he that biddeth him God speed is partaker of his evil deeds" (2 John 10, 11).

We are not being rude or uncouth when we obey God's Word. We are acting in wisdom, realizing that error is a spiritual disease with lethal potential.

False Doctrine Is Powerful

The Bible portrays spiritual error as a strong and overcoming force. Once it gets hold of an individual, it can control that person's being. The author of Hebrews warned, "Be not carried about with divers and strange doctrines" (Heb. 13:9). Paul explains that false views destabilize one's understanding, filling it with doubt, like a befuddled child. Then it sweeps him off his feet and carries him away captive. He wrote: "That we henceforth be no more children, tossed to and fro, and carried about with every wind of doctrine, by the sleight of men, and cunning craftiness, whereby they lie in wait to deceive" (Eph. 4:14).

The power of error also explains why so many involved in

non-Christian religions can be so zealous. They have been overcome by the power of error. Jesus illustrated this: "Woe unto
you, scribes and Pharisees, hypocrites! for ye compass land and
sea to make one proselyte, and when he is made, ye make him
twofold more the child of hell than yourselves" (Matt. 23:15).

Many are convinced that error is truth. They make astonish-
ing sacrifices to advance their cause. Mormons dedicate whole
years of their lives to sharing their faith. Jehovah's Witnesses
dedicate their entire lifetimes to the spreading of their beliefs.
They are sincere and zealous—but dreadfully wrong. Paul
spoke of the Jews as those who "have a zeal of God, but not
according to knowledge" (Rom. 10:2). Hodge comments:

> No practical mistake is more common or more dangerous
> than to suppose that all zeal about God and religion is neces-
> sarily a godly zeal. Some of the very worst forms of human
> character have been exhibited by men zealous for God and his
> service; as, for example, the persecutors both in the Jewish and
> Christian churches. Zeal should be according to knowledge
> (C. Hodge 1972, 343).

The power of error is even greater, more blinding, than the
power of immorality. Again Hodge notes:

> Error is often a greater obstacle to the salvation of men than
> carelessness or vice. Christ said that publicans and harlots
> would enter the kingdom of God before the Pharisees. In like
> manner the thoughtless and sensual Gentiles were more sus-
> ceptible of impression from the Gospel, and were more fre-
> quently converted to Christ, than the Jews, who were wedded to
> erroneous views of the plan of salvation (C. Hodge 1972, 331,
> 332).

At least as great care, then, should be expended on preserving oneself from error as it is in keeping oneself from immorality. Many an adulterer, thief, and embezzler have been won to
the Lord. But, in comparison, how many religious zealots forsake their error to embrace the way of the cross?

And what is the sad end of all the zeal that is misplaced on unbiblical beliefs? The Lord reveals:

> Woe unto them that call evil good, and good evil; that put darkness for light, and light for darkness; that put bitter for sweet, and sweet for bitter! . . . Therefore as the fire devoureth the stubble, and the flame consumeth the chaff, so their root shall be as rottenness, and their blossom shall go up as dust: because they have cast away the law of the LORD of hosts, and despised the word of the Holy One of Israel (Isa. 5:20, 24).

Woe. Sadness. Futility. Despair. Our hearts go out to those thus blinded. We must ardently pray for their conversion, doing whatever we can lawfully do to help them, keeping in mind the danger of being contaminated with their error. Jude captures this blend of compassion and contagion when he counsels, "And others save with fear, pulling them out of the fire; hating even the garment spotted by the flesh" (Jude 23).

Little errors lead to more serious error. The Christian should develop the discipline of scrutinizing every doctrine in the light of God's Word. The spiritual health of Christianity would be advanced if the practice of the Bereans widely operated today: "These were more noble than those in Thessalonica, in that they received the word with all readiness of mind, and searched the scriptures daily, whether those things were so" (Acts 17:11).

How dangerous is false doctrine? It is so dangerous that contact with it is to be shunned. It is so deadly that few engulfed by it are rescued. As Hodge warns: "Let no man think error in doctrine a slight practical evil. No road to perdition has ever been more thronged than that of false doctrine. Error is a shield over the conscience, and a bandage over the eyes" (C. Hodge 1972, 332).

14

What Are
the Signs
of Apostasy

?

There are many ways to express the truth, not all of which are beneficial. "The tongue of the wise useth knowledge aright" (Prov. 15:2). To use knowledge rightly is to use it in a humble spirit for the assistance of others. It is to speak "the truth in love" as Paul commanded (Eph. 4:15). Solomon contrasts the right and wrong uses of knowledge as follows: "There is he that speaketh like the piercings of the sword: but the tongue of the wise is health" (Prov. 12:18).

It has been the great desire of my heart, in writing this book, to heal, not to sever. I have sought to instruct and not to offend. I, at times, have used stern and arousing language only because I deeply believe there is great cause for alarm.

The Bible speaks of the great apostasy that will precede Christ's second advent (2 Thess. 2:3), an apostasy that will affect multitudes of people. The word *apostasy* signifies the abandoning of something once firmly believed. It appears evident to me that the seeds of that great prophetic departure are

142

being sown deeply in the church by means of false doctrine and the mystical experiences it produces.

The road to apostasy, however, is not limited to the pathways marked by the neon signs of satanic miracles and false prophets. There are other roads that lead away from the historic Christian faith. Down the road they will all converge into one giant superhighway of apostasy. For a while these roads are small and seem rather safe. They are not traveled by the godless throngs. Nevertheless, they are dangerous roads marked by certain signs. And when these signs appear, the traveler is in peril.

Physical versus Spiritual

One way leading perilously away from God is where the physical is stressed rather than the spiritual. Jesus gave a central truth when he declared, "God is a Spirit: and they that worship him must worship him in spirit and in truth" (John 4:24).

God warned Samuel: "Look not on his countenance, or on the height of his stature; because I have refused him: for the LORD seeth not as man seeth; for man looketh on the outward appearance, but the LORD looketh on the heart" (1 Sam. 16:7).

As physical beings we have a tendency to concentrate on that which is visible. How easy it is to think that physical prosperity is a certain sign of God's blessing. But Paul warns that one of the teachers from whom we should withdraw ourselves is the one who teaches "that gain is godliness" (1 Tim. 6:5). Big is not always best. New is not necessarily better than used.

This was the great error of ancient Israel. They stressed the physical rather than the spiritual. The circumcision of the flesh became the mark of sainthood rather than the circumcision of the heart, outward sacrifices rather than inward worship (see Deut. 10:16; Jer. 4:4; Isa. 1:11–18; Micah 6:6–8; 1 Sam. 15:22).

The church of the Laodiceans (Rev. 3:14–22) was an apostate church. They were rejected by Christ, "the faithful and true witness" (vv. 14, 16). Why were they rejected? Jesus said,

"Because thou sayest, I am rich, and increased with goods, and have need of nothing; and knowest not that thou art wretched, and miserable, and poor, and blind, and naked" (v. 17).

It is a sign of peril when man's eyes are directed to the physical sphere as if it were the primary sphere. This can subtly happen when a preacher begins to emphasize property, prosperity, or politics rather than the kingdom of God (see Matt. 6:31–33; 2 Cor. 4:18).

The great southern theologian R. L. Dabney (1820–1898), though he was a Confederate officer, lamented the tendency in his day to drag politics into the pulpit. He warned:

> God has reserved for our spiritual concerns one day from seven, and has appointed one place into which nothing shall enter, except the things of eternity, and has ordained an order of officers, whose sole charge is to remind their fellow-men of their duty to God. . . . But when the world sees a portion or the whole of this sacred season abstracted from spiritual concerns, and given to secular agitations, and that by the appointed guardians of sacred things, it is the most emphatic possible disclosure of unbelief. It says to men, "Eternity is not of more moment than time; heaven is not better than earth; a man is profited if he gains the world and loses his soul". . . . We solemnly protest to every minister who feels the impulse to introduce the secular into his pulpit, that he thereby betrays a decadent faith and spiritual life in his own breast. Let him take care! He is taking the first steps toward backsliding, apostasy, damnation (Dabney 1979, 42, 43).

Cause versus Character

The second road leading away from God is the one in which a cause is stressed over character. There are many important causes or issues that warrant our attention and action. But none of these should become ends in themselves. How many times have people become so caught up with a cause that they can justify anything as long as it is done for the cause?

Saul of Tarsus was so devoted to the cause of exterminating Christianity that he could justify imprisoning or even killing male and female Christians (Acts 9:1, 2). He did this even though his conscience hurt him (v. 5). The cause had overcome his conscience.

When the Israelites were fighting the Philistines, they had a tremendous cause (see 1 Sam. 4–7). Unfortunately, they were being trounced by the heathen. To help their cause, the elders of Israel decided to bring the ark of the covenant into the camp. Now they thought that God *must* help them; he certainly would not allow the ark to be taken. But the ark was taken, and the sons of the high priest along with a great multitude were slain. It was not until Israel put away the strange gods and returned to the Lord (7:3) that God delivered them from the Philistines. Character is more important to God than all of our causes.

The church of Ephesus (Rev. 2:1–7) had been faithful in maintaining some very important causes. They had labored hard and long in these causes. They patiently had confronted error and false apostles in Christ's name (v. 3). Nevertheless, Jesus said, "I have somewhat against thee, because thou hast left thy first love" (v. 4).

So serious was this character deficiency, in the eyes of Christ, that he warned them: "Remember therefore from whence thou art fallen, and repent, and do the first works; or else I will come unto thee quickly, and will remove thy candlestick out of his place, except thou repent" (v. 5).

Doctrinally, the Ephesians were sound; but that would not preserve them from apostasy if they lost the motivating unction of love to Christ. This is the great warning to those of us called fundamentalists. It is possible for the cause of church purity to digress into a cycle of endless separations ending in total isolation. The spirit of harsh, unloving criticism is wrong. Doctrinal and ecclesiastical purity are important. But they cannot rightly function apart from a heart of love.

Exclusiveness versus Evangelism

Another road to apostasy occurs when Christians forget the Great Commission of Christ to "Go ye into all the world, and preach the gospel to every creature" (Mark 16:15). Instead of turning outward with the light of salvation, some turn inward. All they can see is themselves, their denomination, their history, their faithfulness. This is the "remnant syndrome." Each part of the body of Christ wants to legitimize its own existence. So they are tempted to stress their own distinctives and heap praises upon themselves. Instead of seeing the lack of church growth around them as distressing, they view it as a badge of honor. "We are God's little remnant. The road to heaven is very narrow and few go in at it. The devil often attacks us, because we are special to God." Such ones will point everywhere with an excuse for their diminishing numbers, except at themselves. They might even blame God's election for their dilemma. Such a testimony will never die from compromise. No. No. But it will die of attrition. And that, too, is apostasy.

Charles Hodge solemnly reminds us:

> In the gift of His Son, the revelation of His Word, the mission of the Spirit, and the institution of the Church, God has made abundant provision for the salvation of the world. That the Church has been so remiss in making known the gospel is her guilt. We must not charge the ignorance and consequent perdition of the heathen upon God. The guilt rests upon us. We have kept to ourselves the bread of life and allowed the nations to perish (C. Hodge 1988, 41).

May God give us all the grace to walk in a way that is worthy of the name Christian, that we would do all things for the glory of Christ, obeying the Word of Christ, being empowered by the Spirit of Christ.

> Now unto him that is able to keep you from falling, and to present you faultless before the presence of his glory with exceeding joy, to the only wise God our Saviour, be glory and majesty, dominion and power, both now and forever. Amen (Jude 24, 25).

Appendixes

APPENDIX **1**

Is the Bible
an Open System

?

I was listening to an eminent New Testament scholar commenting on some serious issues facing the church today. I was truly blessed through his thorough, deep, and practical understanding of the New Testament. His exegetical comments were impelling. Later I was able to talk with him. I expressed my belief that the church could greatly benefit from his insights. Then I frankly asked him if he had ever considered publishing a work that would deal with an exegetical investigation of the question in debate. I was floored by his response. Roughly, his reply was:

When I studied for my Ph.D., I was stripped of all dogmatism. My mentors showed me there were many possible ways of look ing at data. Each of these points of view has merit. They insisted that this applied to theology and to biblical interpretation. The moment I would assert something to be factual or conclusive, they would shoot it down. They did not disprove it, but they raised enough doubt in my mind that I could no longer be

dogmatic. I fear that I lost more than I gained. I gained a doctoral degree, but I lost some of my cherished convictions.

The dilemma faced by that man as a doctoral student was
the result of a dramatic change which has occurred in the
scientific world. The recent shift in scientific method has been
away from the concept of laws and toward the concept of models. Formerly, the study of science would lead to absolute statements. These were viewed as fixed laws of truth, and the
systems they composed were termed closed or comprehensive.
This scientific dogmatism was accepted because most scientists believed they were objectively studying all the possible data
related to their area.

As scientific advancements multiplied and the tools available
for scientific investigation became more sophisticated, old
theories were forsaken. Scientists began to realize, with the aid
of advanced tools like microscopes, telescopes, space and ocean
exploration, computer and laser technology, that systems pre-
viously declared closed were still very much open. Old theories
began to explode as new data was gathered.

The simple fact was that all the data had not been observed
prior to the system being "closed." With each new scientific
discovery, the field of exploration is increased and new data
must be tested and integrated into scientific theory. Hence, it is
no longer safe to be dogmatic except in some fields like simple
mathematics, which obviously is a "closed" area.

The age of models has come. A model takes the place of a law.
Models are human perceptions of truth. They are tentative and
thus subject to change as new data becomes available. These
models are open and constantly tested. No scientist dares claim
any longer that one model is the way to explain all known
phenomena for fear that some newly discovered data will prove
that scientist to be a precipitous fool. The world of science has
progressed from the old approach (closed systems) to the new
approach (open systems).

Truth is still obtainable to the scientist. The way to arrive at it is more laborious, to be sure. And once a theory has been well-tested, it is not proudly asserted to be the final word. This approach is fine in the areas of natural and behavioral science where the horizons of study are constantly expanding. But what happens when this approach to truth is applied to the science of hermeneutics (the interpretation of the Bible)?

The result is devastating. The quest for truth would never be completed. Neither moral nor theological absolutes would be obtainable. The Bible's message could no longer be declared with authority if it were an "open system." If new inspired revelations were still being given by God for the faith and life of the church, then the very foundation of our faith would be eroded, because truth would not yet be finalized. Despite these catastrophic results, some professing evangelical scholars are adopting this approach. In their writings we read of biblical models instead of biblical law. See Charles Kraft's *Christianity in Culture* (Orbis, 1979) as one advocate of this change, and William Larkin's *Culture and Biblical Hermeneutics* (Baker, 1988) for a thorough refutation of it.

I believe that men like Charles Kraft have made a tragic mistake. In their attempt to stay up-to-date, to utilize new scientific methods in their approach to hermeneutics, they have unintentionally adopted a paradigm that effectively threatens the simple faith of millions. If the Bible is a closed system of truth, with no new revelation being given through inspired prophets or apostles, then the "model approach" is an erroneous and dangerous tool in hermeneutics.

There should be no confusion in this area. The orthodox teaching of Christianity has always affirmed that God's special, saving revelation to mankind is restricted to the teachings of the Scriptures. As stated in the Westminster Confession of Faith: "The whole counsel of God, concerning all things necessary for his own glory, man's salvation, faith, and life, is either expressly set down in Scripture, or by good and necessary consequence may be deduced from Scripture: unto which nothing at any time is to be added, whether by new revelations of the Spirit or traditions of men" (I:6).

This is the issue. If the Bible is complete, then it represents a closed system of truth. If it entails a fixed and absolute standard of truth, then the teachings of Scripture may be ascertained and dogmatically asserted. If God is still granting new revelation, then the truth of God is still being progressively revealed, and if this were the case, our duty would be to faithfully listen to today's prophets as they unravel God's truth in new and clearer representations than we find in Scripture. Few Christians really consider the subtleties of today's "prophets" as an improvement upon the sanctifying truths given in the Word. I certainly do not.

The modern concept of models is just not applicable to a closed system of truth. No one will ever prove that $1 + 1 = 3$. Simple mathematics is a closed system of truth. $1 + 1 = 2$ is a law, not a model. So, to allow the new scientific method to strip us of our theological convictions is a tragedy. The new scientific approach cannot be applied to a closed system. And the Bible is a closed system of divine truth.

APPENDIX **2**

Is There Healing
in the Atonement

?

On this question there is great division in the church today. The two sides of this issue are normally the charismatic and the noncharismatic. The former declares that Christ's atoning work was as much for sickness as it was for sin, so the believer should accept Christ not only as his sin bearer but also as his sickness bearer. The noncharismatics usually take the position that Christ's death was for sin and did not relate directly to physical sickness. Those Scriptures that speak of our being healed by his stripes or his death refer to spiritual, not physical healing.

Hence, the charismatics do believe that there is physical healing in the atonement, whereas the others do not believe there is promise for physical healing in Christ's atonement.

I would like to submit B. B. Warfield's following statements as a strong argument that neither side is totally right nor wrong. He was answering the position of faith healers in his day when he said:

This error does not lie in the supposition that redemption is for the body as well as the soul, and that the saved man shall be renewed in the one as well as in the other. This is true. It lies in confusing redemption itself, which is objective and takes place outside of us, with its subjective effects, which take place in us; and in failing to recognize that these subjective effects of redemption are wrought in us gradually and in definite order. . . . Here, you perceive, is a process. Even after we have believed in Christ, and have a title as justified men to the benefits bought for us by His blood and righteousness, entrance into the actual enjoyment of these several benefits remains a process, and a long process, to be completed in definite order. This is true of the spiritual blessings which come to us through the atonement of Christ. We are no longer under the curse of sin. But we remain sinners. . . . We have not yet obtained, and we are not yet made perfect.

It is little that we continue also physically weak, liable to disease, and certain to die. For the removal of these physical evils, too, provision is made in the atonement. But the benefit here too is not received all at once. For us, as in the broader sphere of the world's salvation, death is the last enemy to be conquered. Though the redeemed of the Lord and no longer under the dominion of sin, the results of sin remain within us: inwardly we are corrupt, outwardly we are the prey of weakness and disease and death. We shall not escape from either in this life. Who is there that sins not? And who is there that does not suffer and die? But ultimately we are relieved from both. . . . This is the teaching of the Bible; and this is what Christ illustrated when He healed the sick in His ministry on earth that men might see, as in an object-lesson, that provision was made in His substitutionary work for the relief of every human ill. There is included in this, however, no promise that this relief is to be realized in its completeness all at once, or in this earthly life. Our Lord never permitted it for a moment to be imagined that the salvation He brought was fundamentally for this life. His was emphatically an other-world religion. He constantly pointed to the beyond, and bade men find their true home, to set their hopes, and to place their aspirations, there (Warfield 1972, 176, 177).

And now let us very briefly sum up from our own point of view what it seems that we ought to think of Faith-Healing. First of all, . . . let it be remembered that the question is not: (1) Whether God is an answerer of prayer; nor (2) whether, in answer to prayer, He heals the sick; nor (3) whether His action in healing the sick is a supernatural act; nor (4) whether the supernaturalness of the act may be so apparent as to demonstrate God's activity in it to all right-thinking minds conversant with the facts. All this we believe (Warfield 1972, 192).

Warfield lists three arguments of faith healing that presuppose or lead to many false doctrines:

(A) Sickness and sin are often connected in an utterly unscriptural manner. That all the sicknesses which afflict our race are a result of sin is true. But that special sicknesses infer special sin our Saviour Himself explicitly denies. (B) These arguments would be equally valid to commend perfectionism. If sinfulness is not to be removed in this life, neither is sickness. Both are the fruits of guilt, and both are removed on the basis of the work of the guiltbearer; and both are removed only when the subjective salvation is completed. (C) They are founded on a completely unscriptural view of the functions of suffering, and the uses of sickness and pain. All sickness and suffering are spoken of as if they were from the evil one alone; as if they were sheerly the mark of the displeasure of God; and as if they were a fruit of particular sin. Scripture says: "Behold whom the Lord loveth He chasteneth, and scourgeth every son whom He receiveth." Sickness is often the proof of special favor from God; it always comes to His children from His Fatherly hand, and always in His loving pleasure works, together with all other things which befall God's children, for good (Warfield 1972, 194).

APPENDIX 3

Is Today's
Tongues Speaking
Divine
or Demonic

?

Once again we enter an area of great polarization. Charismatics, of course, believe that their glossolalia is a gift of the Holy Spirit. Many noncharismatics have ascribed demonic agency as the source behind the so-called tongues speaking. It is important to remember the rule that no higher cause be affirmed to an effect than that which is able to produce it. With this rule in mind, a third possibility arises: today's alleged tongues speaking may be neither divine nor demonic; it might be purely human in its source.

Dr. John P. Kildahl conducted a ten-year research on today's alleged speaking in tongues. He wrote a book following his study, entitled *The Psychology of Speaking in Tongues*. His extensive study led him to the following conclusion: "I am therefore advancing the hypothesis that glossolalia is a learned experience, and that these five factors constitute the steps in the learning process" (Hamilton 1975, 131).

The five elements of this process of induction, according to Kildahl, are:

> First, the person who is about to speak in tongues has a great sense of personal distress, often called an existential crisis. In his distress, he is openly seeking and is open for someone who will tell him what to do and provide relief from his suffering. Second, he is generally drawn to a person whom he trusts or eventually comes to trust. In his sense of weakness and dependency, he looks for a person with certainty, for someone who has a sense of definiteness and strength. Third, the charismatic leader is surrounded by a supporting group of fellow believers. The credibility of the leader is enhanced by the presence of this group of followers, who are almost equally firm in their convictions that a solution and an end to suffering lies in following their own path. Fourth, a comprehensive rationale is offered to the initiate to explain what tongue-speaking is, and how it may be understood. Fifth, there is an intense emotional atmosphere at some point in what I have come to call the induction process (Hamilton 1975, 128, 129).

The following statements help to show how alleged glossolalia might be nothing more than a natural motor response made under a state of mental neutrality:

> The capability of being hypnotized and the capability of speaking in tongues are closely related.
>
> Tongue-speakers begin to speak in tongues through the help and direction of a leader who actively initiates the neophyte into the experience. It appears essential that the initiate develop a deeply trusting and even submissive relationship to the person who is his or her mentor. If the initiate holds back, if he is only partly involved in the experience or has strong reservations about the credibility of the leader, then he or she will not begin to speak in tongues. If, for example, a group of twenty persons are exposed to a charismatic leader, those persons in the group who trust the leader the most have the best chance of becoming glossolalists. In subordinating one's own ego to that of the authority figure, the initiate is able to regress psychologically to a level of childlike openness, dependency, and suggestibility.

The ability to submit oneself to a mentor appears to be a precondition for speaking in tongues. This capacity to regress exhibits the same general traits as the trait of hypnotizability. Hypnotizability requires that one be trusting enough to turn himself rather fully over to someone else and to place one's momentary destiny in the hands of the other person. Some persons tend to hang on to their own psychological controls and do not develop the trusting relationship which is the precondition for hypnosis. However, many persons who at first cannot give themselves up will gradually come to trust the mentor and in time will allow themselves to regress enough to be hypnotized.

Hypnotizability constitutes the sine qua non of a glossolalia experience. If one can be hypnotized, then one is able under proper conditions to learn to speak in tongues. While people who speak in tongues are not hypnotized, the induction of glossolalia is very similar to the induction into hypnosis. There is a further connection. After a person has been hypnotized for the first time, it becomes increasingly easy for him to be hypnotized on repeated occasions. This holds true also for the tongue-speaker. Once he has begun to speak in tongues under the conditions of a trusting dependence and regression in the face of the mentor, then the tongue-speaker himself is able to repeat the tongue-speech without repeated induction efforts by the mentor. Once the tongue-speaker has been able to regress and let go of the conscious controls so that glossolalia is produced, then it is easy for him to repeat the same or similar sounds under a wide variety of conditions, whether kneeling in the quiet of a church or driving along the freeway (Hamilton 1975, 131, 132).

However inadequate this explanation may be to the charismatic, it provides for noncharismatics a very plausible explanation of the experience of glossolalia without having to go to the extreme of ascribing demonic agency. It should be noted that the chance of demonic activity is definitely increased when someone willingly regresses into a state of mental suspension. We are made in the rational image of God, and he desires us to increase that aspect of our being by growth in knowledge and faith. We should never diminish it by a leap into the dark. The service of God is always "our reasonable service" (Rom. 12:1).

APPENDIX **4**

What Do Charismatics, Catholics, and the WCC Have in Common

?

I recently heard a charismatic scholar talking about the massive Evangelization 2000 thrust of the Roman Catholic church. The speaker alarmed me when he affirmed, "We must approach the Roman Catholic Church in a totally new way. We should consider Roman Catholics no differently than we would consider Methodists, Presbyterians, or Baptists. They are just another denomination of Christianity." Following his address, there was time for questions. I asked him, "Would your cordial approach to Roman Catholicism be the same if you did not share the common experience which you call the baptism of the Holy Spirit?" His response was a quiet, "Probably not."

David du Plessis, affectionately regarded as "Mr. Pentecost" among charismatics, often told the story of how the Lord gave him the specific vision and command to cooperate with Roman Catholicism in his ministry. He "prophesied" how the mighty work of the Holy Spirit was going to set at nought the doctrinal differences between Protestants and Catholics effecting unity. The charismatic movement now embraces Roman Catholics with total openness. Basic differences of doctrine no longer seem to matter. Huge charismatic meetings feature Protestant and Roman Catholic speakers as if there were no difference between them. Tongues, prophecies, healings abound in such meetings—all with loud and united shouts of "Amen" and "Praise Jesus."

Evangelization 2000 is a project in which the Roman Catholic Church will spend one billion dollars for a decade of evangelization (1990s). The enormous thrust is being headed by Father Tom Forrest, a charismatic Catholic who is treated with utmost respect in charismatic circles. The thrust will culminate with a worldwide satellite telecast on Christmas Day A.D. 2000 when the Pope will address an audience estimated at five billion people. The purpose of Evangelization 2000 is "to give Jesus Christ a 2000th birthday gift of a world more Christian than not." Many professing evangelicals will wholeheartedly support this endeavor.

An example of this occurred at the North American Congress on the Holy Spirit and World Evangelizaton, held in New Orleans in the summer of 1987. Fifty-one percent of the 35,000 in attendance were Roman Catholic. The leading charismatics were all present. Tom Forrest gave the final address of the five-day conference. I have listened very carefully to a tape of his message. He was often interrupted with loud cheering, especially when he spoke of the need to unite as Protestants and Catholics in the evangelization of the world by the year 2000. And the congress' chairman, Vinson Synan, said, "If you want to see something beautiful, come see a Spirit-filled Catholic mass."

The World Council of Churches is a conglomeration of churches without any steadfast allegiance to the Word of God. Liberation theology with its Marxist presuppositions is openly advocated in the council. Guerilla movements advocating violent revolution have received financial assistance from the WCC. The Vancouver World Congress (1983) welcomed animists, Hindus, Muslims, and Buddhists in a celebration of "worship" with its constituents. Nevertheless, the charismatic movement and a growing number of evangelicals continue their strong ties and cooperation with the WCC.

This whole current situation leads to many questions. Do devoted Protestants and Catholics share a common faith? Is there anything wrong with interfaith worship services? Is ecumenical unity the will of God for us today? Should we forget differences in doctrine and emphasize likenesses in experience? Could the devil really be involved in something as moving and life changing as the meetings in New Orleans? Does the Holy Spirit bless and empower those who teach error? Most of these questions have been answered in the body of this book.

The Bible speaks often of the importance of the purity of worship. Jesus twice cleansed the temple with the declarations that the worship of God must not be adulterated. Paul forbade the fellowship of believers with unbelievers (2 Cor. 6:14–16), commanding, "Wherefore come out from among them, and be ye separate, saith the Lord, and touch not the unclean thing; and I will receive you" (v. 17). Christians are told, "And have no fellowship with the unfruitful works of darkness, but rather reprove them" (Eph. 5:11). Solomon attested, "The sacrifice of the wicked is an abomination unto the Lord; but the prayer of the upright is his delight" (Prov. 15:8). The spirit of unity at any price is anti-Christian, because it is opposed to the Word and nature of God.

The unity that Scripture encourages, and for which Jesus prayed in John 17, is the "unity of the Spirit" (Eph. 4:3) and "the unity of the faith, and of the knowledge of the Son of God" (Eph. 4:13). This is true biblical ecumenicity. It is a fellowship forged around the Spirit of God and the Word of God. Any other unity is a spiritual compromise and thus displeasing to our God of truth.

The common denominator between the charismatics, Roman Catholics, and WCC is a mystical experience and an insatiable longing for unity. The danger of this unholy alliance cannot be overstated. The end of it will be confusion and judgment.

Can Christians
Be Demon Possessed

?

Our terms must be adequately defined prior to answering this question. First, what is a Christian? Second, what is meant by demon possession? Until these points are established, consensus is impossible.

The question is not, Can professing Christians be demon possessed? Everyone would agree that they can be. The question is not, Can Christians be demonized? To be demonized is to be affected by demons. The Bible clearly reveals demonic attacks upon Christians, with varying results of ensuing success.

The question restated in more specific terms is, Can born-again Christians be inhabited by demons to the extent where deliverance is attained only by exorcism? This is the true question now dividing many Bible believers.

An increasing number of prominent Christians are reportedly changing their minds and answering Yes to the question (Wagner 1988, 192–196). The reason they are changing their minds is not because of a new understanding of Scripture. It is because of their own personal experiences. They have become involved in exorcising demons from people whom they are convinced are truly born again.

I believe that the crux of the issue reverts back to the question, "What is a Christian?" I personally do not believe truly born-again Christians can be so inhabited by demons necessitating an exorcism. I see the problem as basically soteriological, that is, relating to the doctrine of salvation.

In chapter 12 I deal somewhat with this problem. I strongly believe that there are thousands of people in evangelical churches who are utterly confused concerning the nature of saving faith. It is very possible that these professing Christians are the ones being currently delivered from inhabiting demons. If this is the case, then following their deliverance they should be immediately and properly evangelized.

Central to the proper declaration of the gospel is the full presentation of Jesus Christ to the sinner. Historically, the church taught that Jesus Christ must be accepted as prophet, priest, and king. The following questions and answers of the Shorter Catechism reveal the wonderful knowledge of Christ in his redemptive work:

Q. 23. What offices doth Christ execute as our Redeemer?

A. Christ, as our Redeemer, executeth the offices of a prophet, of a priest, and of a king, both in his estate of humiliation and exaltation.

Q. 24. How doth Christ execute the office of a prophet?

A. Christ executeth the office of a prophet, in revealing to us, by his Word and Spirit, the will of God for our salvation.

Q. 25. How doth Christ execute the office of a priest?

A. Christ executeth the office of a priest, in his once offering up of himself a sacrifice to satisfy divine justice, and reconcile us to God, and in making continual intercession for us.

Q. 26. How doth Christ execute the office of a king?

A. Christ executeth the office of a king, in subduing us to himself, in ruling and defending us, and in restraining and conquering all his and our enemies.

Down through the years the church has slowly whittled away at the full presentation of Christ to the sinner. Today it is common that Jesus be presented only as the sinner's priest or mediator. The full work of redemption is thereby narrowed into "accepting Jesus as Savior." This information is vital for salvation. Christ, the sin bearer, is the heart of the Gospel. But Jesus is more than a sin bearer.

He is also a divine prophet, revealing unto us by his Word and Spirit the will of God. We should accept Jesus as our guide and teacher, then, as well as our Savior. We should come to him with a humble and teachable spirit.

Christ is also King of kings and Lord of lords. Hence, he should be accepted as Lord, for that is who he is. The confession of Christ as Lord was the declaration given at baptism in the early church. The denial of Christ as Lord was all that Roman persecutors demanded of the Christians in exchange for their lives.

It is about time that the church rebelled against the incessant paring away of Christ's person and work. Some people today differentiate between receiving Christ as Savior and receiving him as Lord. They brand their opponents as teaching "Lordship Salvation." I find that designation extremely repugnant, as it misrepresents the issue. Those emphasizing Christ's lordship are not saying that people are unsaved until they show the effects or fruits of Christ's reign in their lives. They are simply affirming that Jesus Christ should be accepted as both Savior and Lord, for this is what the Bible demands (see Matt. 7:21–23; 16:24–26; Luke 6:46; 19:27; Acts 16:31; Rom. 10:9; 14:7–9; Phil. 2:5–11). And whenever this is truly done, the fruit of the Spirit of God will, in time, be evidenced in people's lives.

It is amazing how much the Spirit of God can do with a little truth. There are many who have been truly born again without knowingly accepting Christ as Lord. Nevertheless, I am sure, the spirit of their hearts was one of submission or yielding to Christ as their King. We must not, then, make it the norm of our witnessing to present an abbreviated Christ to the sinner. The more knowledge of Christ that is given, the more stable the convert's faith will be.

The lordship of Christ over his children implies his rule and reign. In Scripture believers are represented as entering into his kingdom at the time of their regeneration. At the same time they are represented as being delivered from the kingdom of Satan—Christ "hath delivered us from the power of darkness, and hath translated us into the kingdom of his dear Son" (Col. 1:13; also Heb. 2:14, 15). And the Christian is declared to be "kept by the power of God through faith unto salvation" (1 Peter 1:5). Paul assured the Philippians, "Being confident of this very thing, that he which hath begun a good work in you will perform it until the day of Jesus Christ" (Phil. 1:6).

True, born again believers are represented as not being "touched" by the evil one because "he that is begotten of God keepeth himself" (1 John 5:18; also John 10:28). Believers persevere and do not give themselves over to demonic possession, by God's grace. This text is referring directly to demonic inhabitation and control. Believers are assured of victory because they are children of God, and the "seed [of God] remaineth in him" (1 John 3:8–10). If Christians can be inhabited by Satan's angels then they are actually the temple of God and of Satan at the same time. Paul asked, "What concord hath Christ with Belial? . . . for ye are the temple of the living God; as God hath said, I will dwell in them, and walk in them; and I will be their God, and they shall be my people" (2 Cor. 6:15, 16).

The teaching of Jesus in Matthew 12:43–45 is pivotal in understanding demonic possession and re-inhabitation. Demons can leave a person and return with greater severity when the demon perceives the person's life to be "empty, swept, and garnished." If Jesus has not been enthroned as Lord and Savior in the person's life, he or she is inhabitable by satanic forces. Moral reformations, professions of faith, and spiritual activity are like cleaning a house. Unless those activities lead to the powerful, regenerating presence of Christ in one's life, the person is susceptible to further demonic control. Where Christ is, the house is not "empty," and Satan cannot inhabit it.

The fact that so many involved in deliverance work deal only with Christians is distressing. The profession of these believers must be carefully tested and proven. I would recommend that no one inhabited by a demon be accepted as a born-again believer. To do so is to relinquish cherished and certain doctrines concerning the Christian's perseverance and preservation. It is a denial of Christ as both the Savior and Lord of his children. It is yet another evidence of capitulating to phenomena, rather than accepting God's Word.

Why Are There So Many Interpretations

?

The fact that there are so many different interpretations of the Bible and resulting denominations of Christians points to a very real dilemma. Some have taken the easy way out by saying that God allows for more than one correct interpretation of his Word. But that clearly is ridiculous. Truth is truth, and error is error. Something cannot be both right and wrong at the same time. There are two simple reasons why there are so many interpretations: the lack of comprehensive study and the lack of following the simple rules of hermeneutics (the science of biblical interpretation).

The Christian can learn some important lessons by observing the physical scientists at work. Many things must be done before scientists believe their theories to be established. They first gather data. Their collecting must be as comprehensive as possible. They cannot shut their eyes to any data, for if they do, their theories will not be conclusive. They are not free to select only the data that support their presuppositions, but must be objective and thorough, or they will be disgraced when their statements are overturned. Scientists then organize their findings into coherent theories that must take into account all the data. They then test and retest their theories in every possible way to prove their accuracy. This is how science has incalculably enriched the world.

Christians must approach their study of the Bible in a similar way. The Bible is their field of inquiry. Its statements are their data. They must be thorough and honest in their study. They must integrate the data into a system of theology that is consistent. The theories of the individual Christian are not to be impressed upon the Bible. Instead, the Bible is to be allowed to speak for itself. We are to yield to its revelation. When the statements of Scripture are comprehensively studied and consistently expressed, Christians can be assured that their understanding is accurate. They know truth. Unlike the scientists, their field of study is not constantly expanding. There are only sixty-six books in the Bible, and this will never change.

It is a simple matter of fact that much disagreement in Bible interpretation has its source in people not doing their research thoroughly. Usually the study has not been comprehensive. Christians stand up and make definitive statements without having considered all the scriptural data. At other times Christians do not consistently integrate their findings with clearly revealed truth. When concepts stand alone, they often seem plausible. The subtle errors involved do not become obvious until the attempt is made to connect them coherently with the doctrines clearly taught in Scripture. A principle cannot be true if its affirmation demands the denial of some clearly accepted biblical truth.

Great danger arises when teachers assert certain errors to be truth. They are so impressed with the discoveries they have made that they do not think through the implications. Of course, they take for granted that they are true. After all, their discoveries are the fruit of their Bible study. But such declarations are tragic, for they involve eternal things. The errors are repeated by the hearers and become points never to be yielded. Divisions necessarily occur when the pretended truths are exposed as error. Pride inhibits the teachers from admitting the mistakes, and their disciples determine to follow their leaders whatever the cost. For this reason the Bible warns us against rashly declaring our opinions to be truth. James advises, "Be not many of you teachers, my brethren, knowing that we shall receive heavier judgment" (James 3:1 ASV).

Another reason for the differences in our understanding of Scripture is that not everyone uses the same rules of interpretation. We should not invent our own way of interpretation, but should use the same rules employed by faithful Christian expositors for centuries. These tried-and-true rules are summarized by Charles Hodge as follows:

1. The words of Scripture are to be taken in their plain historical sense. That is, they must be taken in the sense attached to them in the age and by the people to whom they were addressed. . . .

2. If the Scriptures be what they claim to be, the word of God, they are the work of one mind, and that mind divine. From this it follows that Scripture cannot contradict Scripture. God cannot teach in one place anything which is inconsistent with what He teaches in another. Hence Scripture must explain Scripture. . . .

3. The Scriptures are to be interpreted under the guidance of the Holy Spirit, which guidance is to be humbly and earnestly sought. The ground of this rule is twofold: First, the Spirit is promised as a guide and teacher. He was to lead the people of God into the knowledge of the truth. And secondly, . . . the unrenewed mind is naturally blind to spiritual truth (C. Hodge 1988, 94, 95).

Employing these rules will assist us in determining the true sense of Scripture. If Christians would constantly unite a thorough investigation with these simple rules, differences of interpretation would practically disappear.

Works Cited

Alexander, A.
1836   *Evidences of the Authenticity, Inspiration, and Canonical Authority of the Holy Scriptures.* Philadelphia: Presbyterian Board of Publications.

1850   *Practical Sermons: To Be Read in Families and Social Meetings.* Philadelphia: Presbyterian Board of Publications.

1967   *Thoughts on Religious Experience.* London: The Banner of Truth Trust.

Alexander, J. A.
1980   *A Commentary on The Acts of the Apostles.* Edinburgh: The Banner of Truth Trust.

Bruner, F. D.
1970   *A Theology of The Holy Spirit.* Grand Rapids: Wm. B. Eerdmans Publishing Co.

Calvin, John
1979   *Institutes of the Christian Religion.* 2 Vols. Translated by Henry Beveridge. Grand Rapids: Wm. B. Eerdmans Publishing Co.

1984   *Calvin's Commentaries.* Translated by John King. 22 Vols. Grand Rapids: Baker Book House.

Chantry, W.
1979   *Signs of the Apostles.* Edinburgh: The Banner of Truth Trust.

Dabney, R. L.
1979   *Sacred Rhetoric.* Edinburgh: The Banner of Truth Trust.

Davis, John D.
1973   *Davis Dictionary of The Bible.* Grand Rapids: Baker
             Book House.

Ensign, G. and Edward Howe
1984   *Bothered? Bewildered? Bewitched?* Cincinnati: Re-
             covery Publications.

Gasson, Raphael
1966   *The Challenging Counterfeit.* Plainfield, NJ: Logos In-
             ternational.

Hagin, Kenneth
1978   *Seven Steps to Receiving The Holy Spirit.* Tulsa, OK:
             Faith Library Publications.

Hamilton, Michael
1975   *The Charismatic Movement.* Grand Rapids: Wm. B.
             Eerdmans Publishing Co.

Hendriksen, W.
1955   *New Testament Commentary. The Pastoral Epistles.*
             Grand Rapids: Baker Book House.

Hodge, A. A.
1976   *Evangelical Theology.* Edinburgh: The Banner of
             Truth Trust.

Hodge, Charles
1851   *The Constitutional History of the Presbyterian Church
             in the United States of America.* Philadelphia: Pres-
             byterian Board of Publications.

1960   *Systematic Theology.* 3 Vols. London: James Clarke &
             Co., Ltd.

1972   *Commentary on the Epistle to the Romans.* Grand
             Rapids: Wm. B. Eerdmans Publishing Co.

1979   *Princeton Sermons.* Edinburgh: The Banner of Truth
             Trust.

1982   *A Commentary on the Epistle to the Ephesians.*
             Grand Rapids: Baker Book House.

1988   *Systematic Theology.* Abridged by Edward Gross.
             Grand Rapids: Baker Book House.

n. d.   *An Exposition of the First Epistle to the Corinthians.*
             Grand Rapids: Wm. B. Eerdmans Publishing Co.

Jorstadt, E.
1973   *The Holy Spirit in Today's Church.* Nashville, TN:
             Abingdon Press.

Kraft, Charles
1979   *Christianity in Culture.* Maryknoll, NY: Orbis Books.

Larkin, William
1988   *Culture and Biblical Hermeneutics.* Grand Rapids: Baker Book House.

Leahy, F.
1975   *Satan Cast Out.* Edinburgh: The Banner of Truth Trust.

Lewis, C. S.
1978   *Mere Christianity.* New York: Macmillan Publishing Co., Inc.

Machen, J. G.
1982   *God Transcendent.* Edinburgh: The Banner of Truth Trust.

Nolen, William
1974   *Healing: A Doctor in Search of a Miracle.* New York: Random House.

Otis, G.
1980   *"Power Encounter: The Way to Muslim Breakthrough."* Evangelical Missions Quarterly 16.

Schaeffer, Francis
1984   *The Great Evangelical Disaster.* Westchester, IL: Crossway Books (a division of Good News Publishers).

Scott, Thomas
1846   *The Holy Bible with Explanatory Notes, Practical Observations and Copious Marginal References.* 3 Vols. New York: W. E. Dean Printer & Publisher.

Unger, M.
1985   *Demons in the World Today?* Wheaton, IL: Tyndale House.

Wagner, C. Peter
1988   *How to Have a Healing Ministry Without Making Your Church Sick.* Ventura, CA: Regal Books (a division of Gospel Light).

Warfield, B. B.
1972   *Counterfeit Miracles.* London: The Banner of Truth Trust.

1976   *Selected Shorter Writings.* Vol. 2. Nutley, NJ: Presbyterian & Reformed Publishing Co.

1981   *The Works of Benjamin B. Warfield.* 10 Vols. Grand Rapids: Baker Book House.

Warner, T.
1986   *"Teaching Power Encounter."* Evangelical Missions
             Quarterly 22.

Watson, Thomas
1970   *The Ten Commandments.* London: The Banner of
             Truth Trust.

Wimber, John
1986   *Power Evangelism.* San Francisco: Harper & Row.

1987   *Power Healing.* San Francisco: Harper & Row.